THE INNER (R)EVOLUTION:

TRAILBLAZE YOUR NEW LUSCIOUS REALITY

DR. CYNTHIA MILLER

CONTENTS

Also by Dr. Cynthia Miller	ix
AUTHOR'S NOTE	1

PART I
THE INNER (R)EVOLUTION

1. OVERVIEW	7
2. CHANGE YOUR LIFE AND REALITY	24
3. THE FEAR BOT	29
4. TRAILBLAZER TECHNOLOGIES AND SOUL CIRCUITRY	63

PART II
DIMENSIONS

5. THE FIRST TWELVE DIMENSIONS	83
6. THE MOTHERBOARD	89
The 1st Dimension - ENERGY	90
The 2nd Dimension – SAFETY	95
The 3rd Dimension – SELF-ACCEPTANCE and LOVE	104
The 4th Dimension – BOUNDARIES	113
7. DREAM BUILDER	126
The 5th Dimension - INDIVIDUALITY and COMMUNITY	128
The 6th Dimension - AUTHORITY	137
The 7th Dimension - CREATIVITY	146
The 8th Dimension - SELF-WORTH and VALUE	156
8. INNER FREEDOM	172
The 9th Dimension - COSMIC AWARENESS	174
The 10th Dimension - INNER MASCULINE	179

The 11ᵗʰ Dimension - INNER FEMININE 184
The 12ᵗʰ Dimension - EMBODIMENT and
FREEDOM 192

PART III
CLAIM YOUR MULTIDIMENSIONAL SOUL SELF

9. PREPARATIONS 205
10. THE PROCESS 216
11. EXPLORING DEEPER 226

PART IV
THE FINAL FRONTIER
Upside Down

12. SPIRALING INTO FORM 245

Acknowledgments 255
Glossary 257
Notes 263
About the Author 269

Gold Dot Publishing
Copyright © 2023 Dr. Cynthia Miller

All rights reserved. No part of this book may be reproduced in any form or by any electronic or mechanical means, including information storage and retrieval systems, without written permission from the author, except for the use of brief quotations in a book review.

The processes in this book are not meant to diagnose, treat, or cure any condition. Please note that this book is not a substitute for medical help. Please consult with your healthcare professional regarding any medical or psychological conditions.

All of the information in this book is published in good faith and for general information purposes only. There is no warranty for the completeness, reliability, and accuracy of this information. Any action that you take based on the information in this book is strictly at your own risk, and we will not be liable for any losses and damages in connection with the information in this book. We are not responsible for your actions.

MMXXIII.1
GoldDotPublishing.com

ISBN: 9780988776364
Cover: Antonio Cesar
Author Photos: MichaelAmici.com
Drawings: Dr. Cynthia Miller
© 2023 Dr. Cynthia Miller

To the girl standing barefoot, in tattered rags in an unknown train station in Iran, 1959. On each hip she held a naked baby with flies crawling in their eyes. She was my age, thirteen, begging for money to survive. When we locked eyes, I looked into her soul, and my life changed.

To the brave souls committed to their awakening, freedom, and the evolution of a new reality.

And to Rose

ALSO BY DR. CYNTHIA MILLER

Unseen Connections: A Memoir from Pain to Joy

The Art of Radical Gratitude

*I Am Worthy; Ignite your Feminine Power -
Self-Help Adult Coloring Book*

AUTHOR'S NOTE

Welcome to The Inner (R)Evolution

I invite you to embark on the most thrilling and fulfilling adventure of your life. Your self-awakening, which leads to creating a new reality, is the ultimate project you will ever encounter, influencing every aspect of your life. Discover who you are and your unseen wonders in twelve miraculous dimensions.

Explore the depth of who you are and reveal why you are on earth at this evolutionary moment. Learn how to change your inner workings, venture into the wilds of transformation, and shift your life. We are on the cutting edge of a quantum leap of consciousness.

Since Inner (R)Evolution is a groundbreaking, radical, and revolutionary new model, it may bump you up against your fears, beliefs, and patterns. We are releasing the old paradigm and stepping into a new reality that supports our sovereignty. For this to happen, the hidden mechanisms of fear, manipulation, and control need to be exposed.

The Inner (R)Evolution is a life-affirming framework for conscious, multidimensional evolution.

> *"All truth passes through three stages.*
> *First, it is ridiculed.*
> *Second, it is violently opposed.*
> *Third, it is accepted as being self-evident."*
>
> - Arthur Schopenhauer, philosopher

Through this book, you may confront new or opposing opinions of what you believe to be true. I encourage you to tune into your guts rather than your preconditioned thinking. How does your body feel? Do the words land true in your inner knowing while your brain flashes red warning signs? I'm not asking you to change your beliefs. Instead, I'm prompting you to explore the possibilities and new worldview presented.

I invite you to read with an open mind connected to the wisdom in your belly, tuning into your inner truth. See what resonates, and explore where my words land. Inspire your left brain to become curious, ignite your creativity and imagination, and trust your guts and inner knowing. Then, implement what you like into your trailblazing practice. Some of my writing is strange and weird; I encourage your uniqueness to come out and play.

Keep rereading. As your neurology and brain shift from reading this book, you will see more layers and dimensions weaving together to create the holographic reality we live in.

Follow me, down the rabbit hole, through the wormhole portal into multiple dimensions of reality, as we venture into uncharted territory traversing the far reaches of the cosmos inside your body.

We are on the precipice of a grand awakening, a new humanity's evolution, and a world of joy, safety, and sustainability for all. I welcome you to proceed with an open mind and generous heart.

I offer this book to you with joy from the depths of my heart and soul.

To your joyful evolution,
Dr. Cynthia

P.S. A few of the terms used in my book, *Unseen Connections: A Memoir from Pain to Joy*, have evolved, and I've changed the names:

• Conscious Multidimensional Evolution, $CM^2=E$, is now The Inner (R)Evolution.
• The Inherited and Childhood Circuit Board is now Childhood Circuitry.
• The OmniFrame or Golden Sphere is now Soul Circuitry.
• Real Self is now the Soul Self.

PART I
THE INNER (R)EVOLUTION

YOUR INNER (R)EVOLUTION

1. OVERVIEW

WE ARE THE VISIONARIES, CREATING A NEW REALITY. Imagine a world that celebrates who you are; your diversity, weird uniqueness, and hidden gifts are welcome.

No more hiding, self-hatred, or lack of self-worth because you don't fit into the prescribed norm of who you are supposed to be. Inner torment and trauma dissolve, self-love blossoms, and your life transforms. You evolve into the person you dream of becoming.

Your life unfolds in multiple dimensions; the pleasure of embodying who you are is the most exciting adventure of a lifetime. You've waited for eons for this time; The Inner (R)Evolution is a portal into a new you and reality.

The greatest secret in life is discovering the truth of who you are. Your most important relationship is the one you have with your body, mind, soul essence, and life-force energy—you.

The journey is clearing out the imposed reality and everything that is not you and expanding into everything that is you—a joyous process of deepening into your being. Life becomes a remarkable project to discover, enjoy and love all the magical, otherworldly, unusual you.

Imagine you're a genetically modified fish, living in a straight cement-lined tank, fed toxic food designed to make you grow a certain way. The purpose of your existence is consumption. That pretty much sums up what's happening on the human level.

Way back in time, we were genetically modified. We live in a straight, constrained worldview and a reality where the Bottom Sludge of humanity's fear, violence, and terror rules the world. The purpose of our existence is to become consumers. Our top-down reality looks like a pyramid where we are controlled to benefit a few. We live in an imposed paradigm that does not sustain our true identity.

This book presents the model, framework, and tools to create an amazing new you and to envision a new reality for the evolution of humanity. An audacious, radical concept. An adventure beyond the forbidden, into the realm of possibility. Based on molecular biology, quantum physics, psychology, and spirituality.

A New Model for Conscious Evolution

The Inner (R)Evolution is a radical approach to healing, transformation, and evolution. I invite you to explore this new model of reality and reconstruct the unseen processes that shape your life. Discover the magic and mystery of navigating and empowering who you are.

Exploring the depth of who you are, reveals why you are on earth at this moment. We are on the cutting edge of a quantum leap of consciousness. This time of profound chaos, deception, and awakening is the perfect opportunity to reinvent a new you and a better world for all.

We are trailblazers, creating a new reality. But the path isn't bushwhacking through the jungle; we are discovering invisible ways to uncover our hidden gifts and share our findings. So it's time to bring out the magical, mystical forbidden treasures—the elixirs of 3-D play you bring to the new reality creation party.

. . .

The Current Reality – The Fear Bot

Humanity is in chaos, in between realities, between the old "normal" and the evolving human. The old paradigm models are no longer applicable; this guidebook shows us how to move forward.

We live in a world where the lowest frequencies of fear, pain, and scarcity rule and are the norm. What's wrong with this picture of reality where we shoot down a classroom of kids, wage war, drop bombs on our neighbors, and sell each other junk food laced with addictive chemicals? This is the old paradigm, also known as patriarchy and colonization, which I've named the Fear Bot. The Fear Bot is the neurological background that creates your current reality.

Fear Bot Reality

The structure of the Fear Bot is the hierarchy, with a few white men on the top and everyone else beneath. The male is supreme, while women and people of color are inferior. Money rules.

This worldview permeates everything, including your neurology, how your body functions, and your DNA. Embedded in everyone's cellular structures, the Fear Bot appears as blocks, challenges, and obstacles designed to keep you small, feeling unworthy, and unloved.

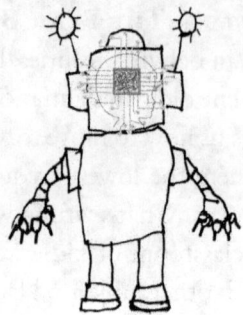

The Fear Bot connects to the lowest frequency in each dimension and links to the Childhood Circuitry.

Childhood Circuitry

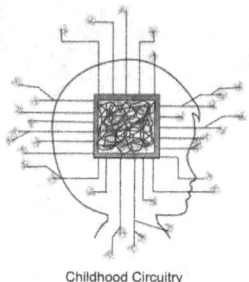

Childhood Circuitry

Created when you were a tiny child, your Childhood Circuitry is the neurological framework of the Fear Bot. Based on other people's ideas and beliefs about you and how you should live, your life functions on patterns that have nothing to do with your soul essence.

You unconsciously experience and live other people's fears, realities, and dreams. To live your dreams, passions, and desires, move your energetic wiring to your Soul Circuitry.

All the deep inner work you have done is great, but until your Childhood Circuitry is rewired, you will always return to your Childhood Circuitry when triggered.

. . .

The Inner (R)Evolution:

SOUL CIRCUITRY

Soul Circuitry

Your Soul Circuitry, a spinning, luminescent, holographic, toroidal energy field, replaces the tangled-up Childhood Circuitry. An energetic framework for merging body and soul and remembering who you are. It's a safe home in all dimensions, a place to heal and regenerate. Soul Circuitry, built to the blueprint of your soul, is alive, fluid, and expands to incorporate all of who you are. When connected to your Soul Circuitry, this is the real you, wise, loving, and creative.

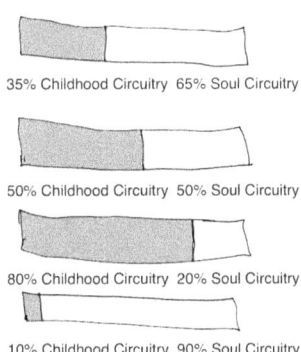

35% Childhood Circuitry 65% Soul Circuitry

50% Childhood Circuitry 50% Soul Circuitry

80% Childhood Circuitry 20% Soul Circuitry

10% Childhood Circuitry 90% Soul Circuitry

Your Childhood Circuitry and Soul Circuitry are on a continuum, with different configurations in each dimension. As you rewire from your Childhood Circuitry and embody your Soul Circuitry, the continuum shifts on each dimension, and you reclaim your body, mind, and soul.

Science shows we can rewire our brains and reprogram our DNA. This book gives you the roadmap to do that and move from your Childhood Circuitry to your Soul Circuitry. New research suggests that the human brain is almost beyond comprehension because it doesn't process the world in two or three dimensions. The human brain understands the visual world in at least eleven different dimensions. As you embody your multidimensional selves, your life and reality evolve into more joyous love and equality for all.

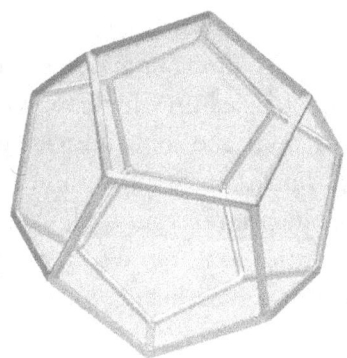

THE FIRST TWELVE DIMENSIONS

The dimensions are not linear; they are like facets on a dodecahedron. A holographic multidimensional field where all the dimensions fit together to create who you are. The dimensions are numbered and presented in sequence, but they are quantum energy fields. As you release the Fear Bot and shift from the grueling challenges embedded in your Childhood Circuitry to your Soul Circuitry's wondrous gifts, your life radically transforms.

. . .

1ˢᵀ Dimension - ENERGY

Your Childhood Circuitry triggers feeling exhausted, sucked dry, others come first, depleted, and you struggle to survive.

Your Soul Circuitry is the framework for your sustainability, an abundance of your soul energy flowing, nourishing your life, and joyous thriving.

How do you choose to direct your energy?

2ᴺᴰ Dimension - SAFETY

Your Childhood Circuitry triggers feeling afraid, scared, unsafe, unprotected, inner battles, mental conflict, beating yourself up, self-abuse, hiding and shrinking to fit in.

Your Soul Circuitry is the framework for your internal security, letting go, expanding, deep breathing, and the safety to be you.

Imagine embodying the safety of enjoying your life, just as you are.

3ᴿᴰ Dimension - SELF-ACCEPTANCE AND LOVE

Your Childhood Circuitry triggers self-hatred, loathing, sickness, negative judgments about yourself, self-disgust, self-sabotage, and comparison to others.

Your Soul Circuitry is the framework for loving your flaws into wholeness, self-acceptance, increased vitality, self-care, health, and delightful self-love.

How can you love yourself more deeply today?

4ᵀᴴ Dimension - BOUNDARIES

Your Childhood Circuitry triggers collective unconscious and subconscious fears and programs that run your life while feeding trauma and suffering.

Your Soul Circuitry is the framework to create boundaries, healing spaces, expansion into more of who you are, and awakening into fun.

Protect yourself with strong, energetic boundaries.

. . .

5ᵀᴴ Dimension - INDIVIDUALITY AND COMMUNITY

Your Childhood Circuitry triggers feeling abandoned, unloved, ostracized, and separate, so you manipulate yourself to fit in.

Your Soul Circuitry is the framework for your authentic self and acceptance of your weird, eccentric, majestic, unique viewpoints; you are seen, acknowledged, and celebrated.

What would it be like to explore being yourself while connected to a loving, supportive, accepting community?

6ᵀᴴ Dimension - AUTHORITY

Your Childhood Circuitry believes in external authority, dogma and doctrine rule, relies on others to show the way, inner doubt, uncertainty, mistrust, shame, and guilt arise, "I'm bad, wrong, unacceptable, or deeply flawed."

Your Soul Circuitry is the framework for self-trust, confidence in your inner knowing and gut wisdom, centered inner authority, and soul essence power.

Where do you want to claim more of your inner authority?

7ᵀᴴ Dimension - CREATIVITY

Your Childhood Circuitry conforms to advertising, mind manipulation, brainwashing, propaganda, indoctrination, social media, TV, the news, fear, and the inner critic that believes your creations aren't good enough,

Your Soul Circuitry is the framework to hold your creativity, unique ways of seeing the world, multidimensional perspectives, soul essence expression, joyous play, and imagining your new life.

Are you ready to shift from living other people's dreams to envisioning your magical life? Be bold, courageous, and creative; add your one-of-a-kind twist and wondrous creations to the tapestry of life.

8ᵀᴴ Dimension - VALUE AND SELF-WORTH

Your Childhood Circuitry triggers feeling worthless, inner poverty, unacceptable, unworthy, inadequate, or insignificant.

Your Soul Circuitry is the framework to hold your self-worth, valuable, abundant, sustainable resources, global health, vibrant eco-system, and a new reality based on cooperation, generosity, and respect.

How can you value yourself more?

9TH Dimension - COSMIC AWARENESS

Your Childhood Circuitry triggers feeling alien, foreign, hiding, pretending to be limited to 3-D, squishing yourself down, and denying your soul essence.

Your Soul Circuitry is the framework to hold your cosmic, magical, connected to the stars, galactic roots, mysterious magical superpowers, and wisdom seen, expand into vast cosmic consciousness.

Planet earth came from the stars; you are made of stardust. So, bring your galactic gifts to the world. (You know you are here to assist in birthing a new reality.)

10TH Dimension - INNER MASCULINE

Your Childhood Circuitry triggers the wounded inner masculine of male dominance, arrogant, superior, thinks he knows best, steals feminine energy, critical, controlling, stuck in his head, cut off from his feminine energies, and emotionally unavailable.

Your Soul Circuitry is the framework to hold your healed inner masculine, who is vulnerable, connects with his feminine essence, creates clear boundaries, charts the direction, hits the mark, and has your back filled with loving, protective support.

How can you love your inner masculine more deeply?

11TH Dimension - INNER FEMININE

Your Childhood Circuitry triggers the wounded inner feminine, stuck in victimhood, waiting to be saved, afraid to trust others, compromises her integrity and values, and squishes her energy, emotions, and power to survive.

Your Soul Circuitry is the framework to hold your healed inner feminine to experience deep safety, vulnerability, and open to receive; she flows her full power, force, and pleasure and births a new life and reality through love, generosity, and joy.

Your inner feminine births all your projects; she holds the keys to evolution, transformation, conceiving a new you, and reality. What are you here to birth?

12TH Dimension - EMBODIMENT AND FREEDOM

Your Childhood Circuitry hides reptilian victim consciousness, deception, lies, and holds a template that scrambles your brain, leaving you feeling helpless, hopeless, and trapped, where you can't distinguish the artificial and victim consciousness from your soul source energy.

Your Soul Circuitry holds all dimensions of you, clarity arises, your soul source energy flows freely, and you claim your neurology, body, self, soul, brilliance, and power, leading to sovereignty, inner liberty, and internal freedom.

Become the person you've always wanted to be; embody all of who you are.

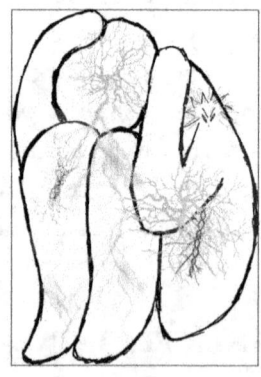

Imagine you grew up in a tiny box. Your neural circuitry conformed to the tight, confining box as you matured. When you release your Childhood Circuitry in twelve dimensions and connect to your Soul Circuitry, every aspect of your life can expand, be seen, and thrive. How you see the world shifts, new possibilities open, and your reality transforms.

Use the Trailblazer Technologies, time-tested, proven multidimensional tools to dismantle, dissolve, and transform the Childhood Circuitry and Fear Bot and move into your Soul Circuitry. In any dimension, discovering the Fear Bot's depth can feel daunting and disheartening.

The Trailblazer Technologies clear the neurological debris, change corrupt DNA codes, and upgrade your body. Experience your exquisite gifts, vision, and brilliance in twelve dimensions. Learn how to create your Trailblazer Practice, the process of claiming your inner freedom and sovereignty.

This book explores multidimensional business and the Final Frontier. Imagine all of your twelve dimensions dancing, exploring your higher frequencies. Your life weaves together in mysterious, exciting new ways. The dread of life turns into joy. Inner peace expands. Contentment and fulfillment grow—your life blossoms.

DR. CYNTHIA MILLER

A Lifetime in the Making

I have an insider's view—direct experience into the depths of how the Fear Bot functions. My father's greatest love was creating nuclear weapons of mass destruction.

During World War II, J. Robert Oppenheimer was in charge of the Manhattan Project at Los Alamos, where Trinity, the atomic bomb, was developed. My dad was the engineer in charge of building Hanford, the weapons-grade Plutonium-239 plant, the fuel necessary to ignite nuclear warheads.

After the war, in 1950, the Cold War between the US and Russia ignited a race to see which country could develop the most lethal weapons the fastest. Oppenheimer took all the scientific research of the Manhattan Project and brought it to Southern California. This information included the physics of Albert Einstein, Edward Teller, Enrico Fermi, Leo Szilard, Ernest Lawrence, Klaus Fuchs, Glenn Seaborg, and others.

Unbeknownst to these scientists, Oppenheimer taught private classes to my dad and three other men at UCLA. Then in a covert, top-secret operation, my dad went to Eniwetok, a remote island in the vast South Pacific Ocean, and directed the construction of the world's first hydrogen bomb.

After thirteen months of supervising the construction, my dad and other top officials sat in Adirondack chairs overlooking the Pacific Ocean, donned goggles, and witnessed the first hydrogen bomb explosion. The deadliest weapon ever invented, 1,000 times more powerful than the bombs dropped on Hiroshima and Nagasaki.

The cataclysmic radioactive electroshock frequencies permanently rearranged my dad's cellular structures and nervous system. Due to his exposure, his body became a radiation transmitter. The next day he flew home after being gone for over a year.

My father's looming presence radiated; energetically, I picked up everything. Then, at dinner, I received shockwaves of radiation frequency. In a flash of seeing, an energetic bomb exploded in the middle of dinner. Even though my five-year-old mind couldn't understand the implications of what I saw, the image was distinct.

With a gigantic burst of light, a massive mushroom cloud grew in the sky, and radioactive particles blew for miles, drifting into the ocean and land. I couldn't figure out how to separate the radiation from the water, soil, and the inside of the plants.

In my innocence, I piped up, "Who will clean up the mess?" I questioned how to remove the radiation from the water and plants. A heavy silence filled the room. He slid back his chair, stood up, pointed his finger at me, and for the only time, sent me to my room.

Hugging my knees, scrunched in the tight space in the corner between the wall and my dresser, I felt alone, frightened, and knew I should keep quiet.

That night triggered the trajectory of my life; an internal spark ignited while I hid in the corner, feeling scared, powerless, and worthless. Even though I was just a girl of no value, I wanted to stop the fear and violence. The imprint of exploding bombs awakened my awareness of the astonishing depth of hatred, torture, and cruelty a few powerful men inflict upon humanity, all cloaked under the guise of peace and freedom.

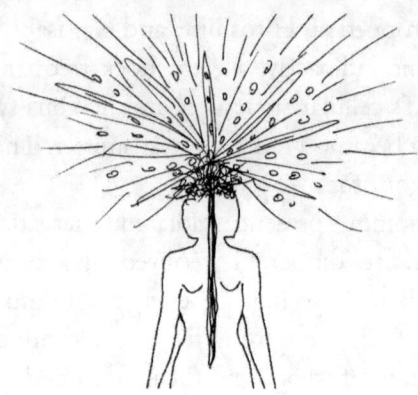

The next level of my insight occurred in 1973 when I was 27. A few days after a near-death experience, a bolt of energy shot up my spine out the top of my head, triggering a spontaneous kundalini awakening. Unknown dimensions appeared; I saw inside bodies, cells, and DNA. I assumed the seeing would diminish, but it remains to this day. My brain and neurons rewired permanently into a new configuration, and my inner seeing and knowing exploded beyond the everyday world into a multidimensional reality.

Whenever I spoke about what I saw, people thought I was nuts. So, I decided to go to graduate school to learn quantum physics, molecular biology, psychology, and spirituality to describe my inner knowing and seeing. My airy-fairy language shifted to acceptable jargon, and I received a Ph.D. in Cellular Transformation and the Psychology of Change. I was 39; it was 1985.

My inner seeing allowed me to work with thousands of clients, rewiring their cellular structures to create miraculous, life-changing transformations. My first clients were sexually abused women whose lives were devastated by the male superiority dogma of the Fear Bot. According to this worldview, the woman was always in the wrong; the man had dominion over a woman's body. It was shocking to see the depth of pain, self-hatred, and trauma held in these women's bodies that impacted every breath of their life until they healed.

FOR DECADES, THE WEIRD EXPERIENCES, INCREDIBLE synchronicities, and multidimensional seeing continued. The Fear Bot wired in my neural structures confirmed that I was a failure, a misfit, and didn't belong. My life looked like a jumbled-up mess. There was no space for all of me to fit into the 3-D definition of being human created by the Fear Bot. I made myself wrong and judged myself for not conforming to the prescribed reality. I tried to deny my inner knowing and seeing. The internal anguish of squishing out parts of myself became unbearable.

Writing my memoir, *Unseen Connections: A Memoir from Pain to Joy*, I realized that each of my weird, unusual experiences took place on a different dimension. The Inner (R)Evolution came to life. An extensive blueprint for the new human, an evolutionary design to manifest a new reality. The map has expanded since writing *Unseen Connections*; it's growing and refining as I learn and evolve.

A lifetime in the making, The Inner (R)Evolution is a profound neurological model of reality that changed my life and the lives of my clients.

How to Use this Book

The Inner (R)Evolution offers a new worldview beyond the scope of the linear sequence of a book. We are creating a multidimensional holographic framework on a flat surface using linear words.

I suggest you read the entire book. You may have questions; keep going. Further chapters will bring more insights and clarity. The image becomes more complex and complete as different layers and dimensions are added. You'll discover amazing things that make sense as you read, but a greater whole will only arise when you finish the book.

Then, once you've read it, reread it slowly. On the second read, you will be able to understand with greater depth and certainty. I invite you to read with your inner knowing, logic, and multidimensional being. Keep yourself open, and feel the essence of what you read.

You may understand things deeply, but sometimes your mind can't picture the whole holographic view. Grasping a multidimensional reality takes time. The more you delve in and read, more profound understanding will arise.

You may be one of the many people who experience a multidimensional reality beyond the norm yet have no context or support for your inner knowing; the Fear Bot denies your inner truth. This book provides a framework for all your eccentric, unspoken experiences, inner knowing, and hidden gifts so that you can thrive.

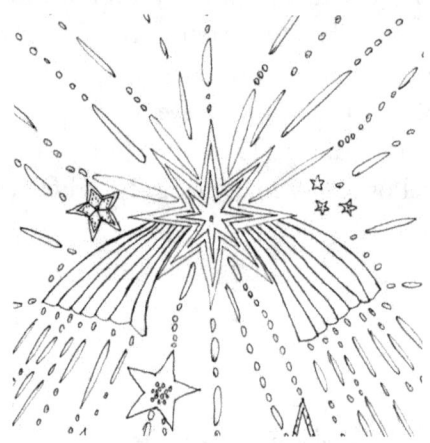

The Future Reality

We are the trailblazers, envisioning and co-creating a new world. We live on the most exquisite planet, yet, we are destroying ourselves and the earth. It's urgent that we consciously evolve before the Fear Bot kills us.

A new grassroots uprising is occurring, celebrating diversity, generosity, and acceptance. A global community, beyond borders and religions, welcomes variety and uniqueness, like the different ecosystems of the earth.

Along with upgrading and transforming your life, you are co-creating our collective future. How you react during this time will have a massive impact on humanity's destiny. You have a piece in creating a new reality.

The repercussions are enormous; each shift in consciousness ripples through your life, out into the cosmos, impacting others and the world. The leap into the unknown takes place inside, trusting your inner knowing, leading to greater health, joy, and freedom to be oneself, and cooperation rather than competition.

Explore your dreams and vision for a new life and worldview. Bring more of yourself to earth to create a beautiful, joyous life. We each have a piece to contribute; your unique vision is essential to create a new tapestry of reality.

The earth is our home, the most spectacular backdrop to create a new reality filled with joy, love, and generosity. By bringing together our multidimensional wisdom and gifts, imagine how we can create a magnificent reality for all.

I invite you on this journey to uncover who you are, change your reality, and thus contribute to humanity's evolution.

Embark on the most joyous, thrilling, luscious adventure, the one you've waited lifetimes to experience. The reason you are here on earth in a body right now.

Welcome to The Inner (R)Evolution

2. CHANGE YOUR LIFE AND REALITY

Change

Change can't happen
so don't tell me
I can transform my life
because it looks like
when I see the world around me
everything seems so crazy
I don't think that
enough change can happen
to make my life and the world a better place.

— Dr. Cynthia Miller

IMAGINE PULLING BACK THE VEILS TO SEE WHAT'S HAPPENING behind the scenes. It's shocking to discover how outside influences orchestrate every aspect of our lives. When the internal mechanisms of fear, manipulation, and control are uncovered and transformed, profound inner freedom and joyous liberation manifest.

(The above poem backward)

The Inner (R)Evolution:

Change

*To make my life and the world a better place
enough change can happen
I don't think that
everything seems so crazy
when I see the world around me
because it looks like
I can transform my life
so don't tell me
change can't happen*

We have been living in the dark, traveling through the jungle of life, cut off from the wisdom, love, and guidance of our soul essence—alone, afraid, struggling through a mysterious illusion.

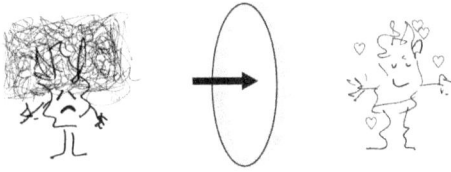

Like all quests and heroes' journeys, the grand adventure into freedom faces risks and challenges while venturing into the unknown. The Fear Bot creates inner torment, a squished self, and a limited reality, which appears as obstacles and challenges. Confront your fears and the Fear Bot to discover new vistas of greater health, inner freedom, and vibrant aliveness. Finally, an ecstatic reunion, coming home to your Self; deep longing fulfilled, luscious, safe space to be all of who you are.

But first, it's imperative to see the forces shaping your reality. Then, you can gain greater sovereignty over your body and life by understanding what is happening behind the scenes.

Years ago, I had a friend who believed in fuckers versus fuckees. According to him, we were fucked over or the ones doing the fucking. So, to save yourself, if you fucked over someone first bad enough, they wouldn't be able to fuck you back. This is the basis of the Fear Bot, a few fucking over the masses to the point where we can't respond.

The fucker-fuckee imprint is rampant. In my father's world, the solution was to bomb and eradicate the fuckees. The fuckees change over time, Japanese, Jews, Blacks, gays, whoever is the current 'others' to exterminate, blame, ostracize, and make wrong. Entire populations fucked over, harassed, and doomed into submission to increase man's domination, power, and wealth.

We are afraid to look inside for fear that we are the torturers. It's easier to assume we are above the brutality. Yet, internally, the Fear Bot inflicts cruelty on ourselves and others. The thought of having to look deeper can be horrifying. On the surface, it's easier to try to escape, but there is no escape; the neurological patterns are inside each of us.

We each have fucker-fuckee programs in our bodies. As we clean up our internal mess, the fucker-fucker program loses energy. The perpetrator/victim cycle is a closed loop; it continues until we break the cycle.

The Inner (R)Evolution:

 → FREEDOM

THE GOOD NEWS IS YOU CAN CHANGE. BIT BY BIT, UNTANGLE and disconnect from the Fear Bot merry-go-round, connect your life-giving energy to your Soul Circuitry on every dimension, exposing your magnificence and brilliance. The magic key to unlock your superpowers is hiding in your neurology.

"Physics professor Vitaly Vanchurin states that we live inside a huge neural network that governs everything around us. It's possible that the entire universe on its most fundamental level is a neural network."[1]

The fabric of the universe is a neural network; we are the neurons, the connectors between the cosmos and earth.

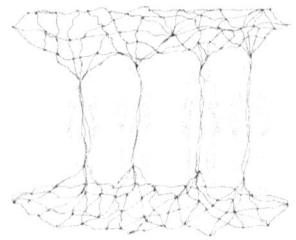

Vanchurin also says, "There are more stable structures (or subnetworks) of the microscopic neural network, and there are less stable structures. The more stable structures would survive evolution, whereas the less stable structures would perish."[2] In my research, the neural networks connected to our soul essence are stable and flourish. On the other hand, the neural networks related to the Fear Bot are collapsing.

Create a new life and reality based on the neural networks of your soul essence instead of the made-up reality of fear and greed. Experience the exquisite joy as your neural circuitry pulsates to the frequencies of the cosmos, earth, and your soul essence.

Your neurology creates your reality; as you shift your neural networks, your life, reality, and the world transform.

I invite you to follow me down the spiraling staircase into the rabbit hole of your neurology.

3. THE FEAR BOT

You've journeyed from the far reaches of the cosmos to be here at this exact moment to assist in the birthing of a new reality. When you signed up for this life, you probably didn't expect to arrive on a beautiful, magnificent planet ruled by money-crazy wacko maniacs.

Are you one of the courageous, bold adventurers here to create a new you and a new reality? If so, it's critical to understand what's happening now in human consciousness.

The Fear Bot is out of control, ready to take over society. The people aligned with the Fear Bot are on a massive campaign to eradicate vast portions of humanity and enslave the rest. The Fear Bot generates a distorted reality of pain, violence, and fear, and is taking over your freedom. By discovering what the Fear Bot is, how it works, and how to use the Trailblazer Technologies, you can bring your magic and gifts to the world.

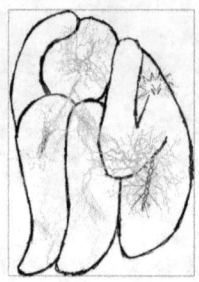

The Fear Bot creates a neurological prison or framework, the inner mechanism that feeds the corruption, brutality, and anxiety that runs rampant today. Like a cage, we live in a structure that keeps us from experiencing and expressing our full, flowing presence. We exist in an exquisite manipulative system rigged against us.

According to the Urban dictionary, a bot is someone that doesn't question the matrix and society as it is. They usually share the same characteristics as robots and AI's. They often run on auto pilot and work a 9-5 and come home to surf their phones and mindlessly open and close Instagram and Twitter.

The Fear Bot is shrouded tight in your neurology; it's hard to detect how deep it goes. You've lived through adversity and have all this amazing inner knowing, but, your nervous system keeps firing the same old patterns, addictions, and self-sabotage programs. The Fear Bot cuts you down to size and keeps you small in a tight box. The Fear Bot pervades humanity.

Current terms that describe the Fear Bot are patriarchy, colonization, the Good Old Boys Network, the old paradigm, Illuminati, Anunnaki, reptilian beings, and victim consciousness. The Fear Bot uses your body and feminine energy as its energy source; without the feminine, it dies.

The Inner (R)Evolution:

Fear Bot Reality

The Fear Bot is designed to create obedient, enslaved people; its purpose is domination, exploitation, and control. To achieve the desired results of massive wealth, authority, and supremacy, the main components of the Fear Bot are:

• A hierarchy where a few people at the top have the power, financial influence, and control of those beneath.
• Men are superior; women are inferior.
• The Fear Bot steals feminine energy to function.
• Money is the basis of reality.
• Fear is the driving force of the Fear Bot.

According to the Fear Bot, money is more important than your body or life. Therefore, you are a commodity used for the financial gain of the elite.

. . .

Money, Hierarchy, and The Fear Bot

The image on the almighty American dollar bill is an excellent example of the hierarchy, superior/inferior concept that runs through humanity. Look at the picture; the top triangle of the select few holds the wealth and all-pervasive seeing. And then there's a gap, with everyone else underneath. So, what happens if, brick by brick, person by person, we stop playing the Fear Bot game?

The belief in a hierarchy as a model of reality is critical to the Fear Bot. The hierarchical model keeps the masses in poverty while women and people of color are at the pyramid's base; a few select white male puppeteers rule.

Allowing a handful of white men to dominate, control, and suck the life and money out of everyone beneath them, is too much to continue to carry. The Fear Bot needs feminine life-giving energy to exist. The Fear Bot's neurological malware in your body lives off your stolen feminine energy. The Fear Bot has no feminine earth energy required to produce anything in the 3rd dimension.

The Inner (R)Evolution:

The Fear Bot is escalating, closing in, grabbing to gain more control, to rule your body, who you can see, and where you can travel.

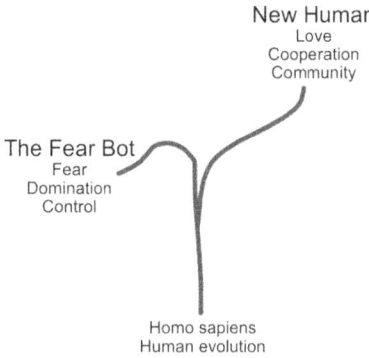

Individually and collectively, we are at a fork in the evolutionary path. Therefore, it's imperative to see what's happening behind the scenes to choose the necessary corrections to thrive.

Reality Bubbles

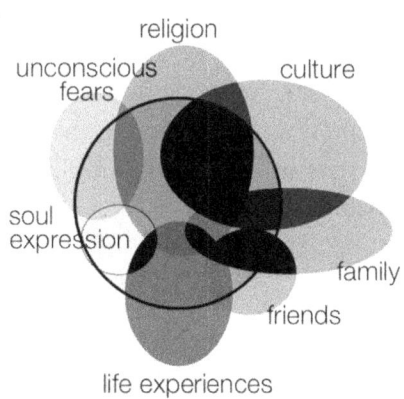

We are led to believe there is a standard one-size-fits-all reality to which we must conform to be accepted and successful—an artificial reality bubble created by the Fear Bot. You live in a reality bubble that dictates how you see the world. Your reality bubble is shaped in childhood, composed of the fake worldview of the Fear Bot.

Each culture, religion, and family have a different reality bubble, a closed system with definite boundaries of acceptable and unacceptable behavior, beliefs, and practices. Add in your life experiences, friends, unconscious fears, and soul expression, and your reality bubble is unique to you. Some of these realities have conflicting opinions, thoughts, and ideas. Internal tension arises when different world views collide inside your body. Most of the conditioning from these realities is unconscious, leading to internal strife, low self-esteem, and fear.

Depression, anxiety, or emptiness take over. The Fear Bot is the force that shapes your reality, interferes with your DNA and nervous system, and creates self-hatred, loneliness, and dread. The Fear Bot functions in all aspects of your life and exists in all dimensions, weaving together and supporting a vast network that holds up the imposed reality. What's wrong with this picture of reality where we shoot down a classroom of kids, drop bombs on our neighbors, and sell each other junk food laced with addictive chemicals?

Discovering the depth of manipulation of the Fear Bot can be daunting and discouraging. All the facets twist together and support each other, creating a robust corrupt neural network in your body beyond the detection of most current technologies. Your neurology creates your reality, which is connected to the Fear Bot that builds the present world.

Let's explore the hidden, crafty, corrupt assistants of the Fear Bot. Then, in the next chapter, we will discover how to use the Trailblazer Technologies to forge your path into your multidimensional joyous self and a luscious sustainable, loving new reality.

The Inner (R)Evolution:

The Fear Bot Cohorts:
- Childhood Circuitry
- Corrupt DNA Codes
- Bottom Sludge
- Nasties
- Beliefs and Thoughts
- Neural Programs
- Veils of Illusion
- The Matrix
- Implants and Brain Clamps
- Trauma

CHILDHOOD CIRCUITRY

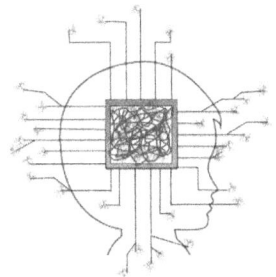

Your Childhood Circuitry was created when you were tiny, and your brain was a sponge and wasn't evolved enough to differentiate between what's yours and what's others'. Unfortunately, your brain can't differentiate between genuine, untrue, and what's best for you.

Your Childhood Circuitry is based on other people's ideas and beliefs about you and how you should live. Parental and societal views to conform to the prescribed norm of the Fear Bot are held in place in the Childhood Circuitry, soldered in, and permanently connected. Your Childhood Circuitry dictates how you feel, what you experience, and how you see reality and the world.

Dr. Bruce Lipton states that we are being programmed for our first seven years of life, and 95% of your life comes from this programming.[1] The majority of these programs are negative and disempowering. After age seven, 95% of your life is orchestrated by that program.

Imagine humanity is a bunch of seven-year-olds waiting for the right Daddy to come and take care of everything: the right political leader, advisor, doctor, or military expert. If we find the right combination of external authorities, everything will be OK. They'll fix everything. But, Big Daddy doesn't care about you. The Fear Bot aims to suck you dry for as long as possible before it kills you off. Your Childhood Circuitry, directly connected to the Fear Bot, keeps the current reality functioning.

We keep reverting to our original programming, the Fear Bot, until we create profound cellular change. A good example is when you go home to your parents' house for the holidays. Your parent's relapse to their old patterns and treat you like a child; you regress to your old behaviors and feelings and get triggered.

The Childhood Circuitry connects to multiple dimensions but is all jumbled together. Layers criss crossing each other, knotted up, create a tangled-up mess of who you are. How you are wired makes it hard to sort out who you are from everyone else.

Not only is your mother's voice in your head, but your great-grandfather's hidden violence is also in your Childhood Circuitry. So, 95% of your life functions on patterns that have nothing to do with your soul essence; your neurology is based on other people's wishes, trauma, and outside influences and has no regard for who you are, your dreams and desires.

Corrupt DNA Codes

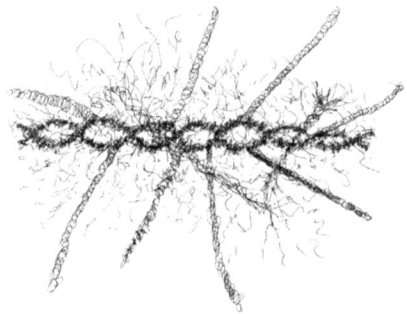

Corrupt DNA codes create the feeling that, deep down, something is inherently wrong with you. On some level, you are unlovable, unworthy, or something unseen is not correct. The corrupt DNA codes are not the truth of who you are.

Some of the corrupt DNA codes go back to humanity's beginning. Wiring malfunctions occurred as humankind evolved. There are different theories, but our DNA was manipulated, tampered with, and re-engineered at some point in our distant history. The Sumerians' ancient clay tablet cuneiform writings dating back to 3200 BCE describe this event.[2] Whether we take these texts as accurate or not, the glitches in the DNA and the neural programs are apparent.

Miniscule strands of DNA curl through our ancestry, picking up unsavory slime. Shadows around the DNA inhibit proper functioning. Our corrupt DNA codes contain the despicable aspects of society and create disease, while sexual abuse and violence patterns pass from generation to generation. In addition, the DNA code is prone to damage and mutations due to errors in DNA replication, free radicals, and radiation exposure.

Like malware on a computer, faulty DNA coding glitches, and malfunctions keep repeating, creating long-range implications, health factors, and genetic predispositions on all dimensions. The corrupt DNA coding also makes viruses spread throughout the environment. The quickest way to manipulate DNA is with a virus; it spreads through the lineage, humanity, and the ecosystem.

About 98.5% of our DNA sequences are called 'junk' DNA. 'Junk' DNA is a term scientists have given to strands of DNA that don't encode proteins.[3] Beyond the scope of current microscopes and instruments, corrupt coding energetically surrounds DNA. Suckers and takers, like leeches and maggots, energetically bind to the DNA and suck off valuable data and energy. Undetectable with the current 3-D technologies, 'junk' DNA holds the information we can use in our internal transformational evolutionary process.

One of the latest scientific technologies is CRISPR, which cuts out chunks of DNA and splices genes together. The scary part about CRISPR is that scientists assume they know what's happening in the cutout and added fragments of DNA. The most advanced equipment only measures and sees the 3rd dimension. Scientists think they know, but the truth is they don't have a clue about the long-term effects.

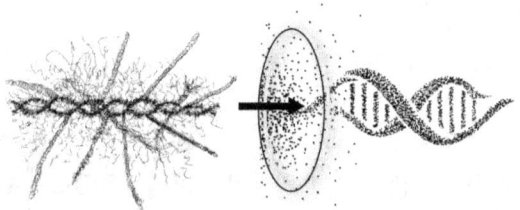

Quantum physics states that everything is energy or frequency. So, using frequency technologies, we can release the corruption encapsulating the codes and clean ancestor shadows traveling on strands of DNA. Current research shows that we can transform our DNA through our high-frequency loving intention and receive profound results. We will explore DNA further in the 2nd dimension.

If you don't understand everything explained here, that's OK; keep reading.

. . .

BOTTOM SLUDGE

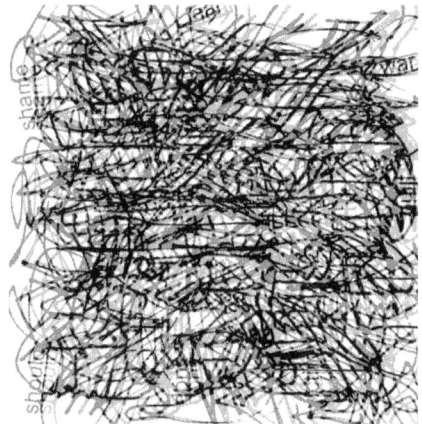

    The Bottom Sludge carries toxic tarry goo and eons of ancient rotting, poisonous debris. Hiding in the most guarded places, the Bottom Sludge of fear and rage covers who you are and why you are here on earth.

    It's scary to venture into the slimy cesspool and observe what you carry in your body. Sticky, gooey tar sucks you down into a cesspool of humanity's unconscious, rotting, stinky crap. Unaware, you become a robot struggling through life, never amounting to much of anything. You're so far into the muck that it's impossible for you to blossom and flourish.

    Bottom Sludge consciousness is the lowest frequency on each dimension that influences your thinking, perception of the world, and life. Each dimension has its unique flavor of self-hatred, self-sabotage, and lies about who you are.

Skipping over the Bottom Sludge leads to more inner torment. Unfortunately, covering internal piles with sparkling golden light does nothing to clear the hidden gremlins and toxic goo. Transformed Bottom Sludge decomposes into energy to fertilize and nourish your dreams.

As you clear Bottom Sludge on each dimension, fear, inner terror, and angst are no longer a part of every breath. There is more space for you, present here on earth. Your higher aspects shine brightly.

Nasties

Do you ever notice dark, yucky energies hanging around? These are the Nasties; they hide and propagate in the Bottom Sludge. Nasties are despicable energies that sabotage, spread a lack of self-worth, and make us dislike ourselves. Nasties appear on all dimensions, thrive on fear, and keep us from evolving. No one is exempt. Nasties spew lies to keep you squished and hating yourself. Nasties like to slink, hide in the shadows, and nip at your heels while devouring your life force.

Imagine encountering vile energies and malware in your body, similar to the characters in Harry Potter, the Hobbit, or Lord of the Rings. There are different agents of the Fear Bot lurking in your body, creating chaos, and making you feel like crap. Nasties have insidious tentacles in every area of our lives. Some are more devastating and destructive than others.

The Inner (R)Evolution:

Sometimes Nasties appear; fluorescent green eyes, spiky hair, and sharp teeth tell you that it's impossible to be loved, that you are despicable scum. Long finger-like tendrils worm their way into every part of your body. "Who do you think you are," bellows an inner voice. "You aren't allowed to do this." The invisible Nasties take over consciousness. "No one will love you; you won't have any friends." The familiar voice protests, "You won't fit in if you go any further."

Some Nasties guard the mechanisms embedded in our ancestry. Nasties scare us into submission; fear keeps the Fear Bot running. The Nasties warn us that it's forbidden to pass beyond their grasp. Their unseen hooks take hold of the nervous system, manipulating how the neural synapses fire and which pathways they follow.

Like fables and old stories, a few of the Nasties, like goblins and ghouls, are the gatekeepers, protecting ancient, hidden gems and unknown treasures.

Sometimes we need to tame the monsters instead of letting them go. It is critical to thank, recognize, and appreciate how long they have been of service. In this gratitude process, we learn much; the monsters become our great friends, protectors in the dark, seers through the muck, and boundary keepers.

Nasties also masquerade as white light. Look closely; it's milky white, opaque, covering ghoulish figures—shapeshifters appearing in many forms. True white light is luminescent and iridescent and emanates love, joy, and pleasure.

Many are waiting for your permission to evolve. Given a choice to evolve, many leave with ease.

Still, others feed the Fear Bot and desire to keep humanity in bondage. Some of these will return to where they came from when given a choice. Others are stubborn, clingy, and refuse to let go. If they stay, melt them with an energetic field of Spiraling Love and Gratitude[4].

The process is simple; the Nasties' low frequency can't survive in the high-frequency Trailblazer Technologies in Chapter 3. Evolve or dissolve; that is their choice.

Claim your body, your life, and your energy. Release those Nasties and watch your awakening and pleasure unfold. The joyous process of expanding into the truth of who you are.

Beliefs and Thoughts

When Emily first came to my office, she could barely walk. Her toes curled up under her feet. Surgeons had cut the back of every toe to straighten them out enough so she could stand. The surgery was successful for a few years, and then her toes crimped up again. After a few operations on each toe, she came to me.

Have you ever looked inside a golf ball and seen those tightly wrapped rubber bands? That is what I saw inside her toes. The tiny rubber bands were thought forms, strings of words. "You'll never amount to anything. You won't stand on your own two feet. You are worthless." Her mother's comments crippled her. She took her mother's words into her body, as we all do.

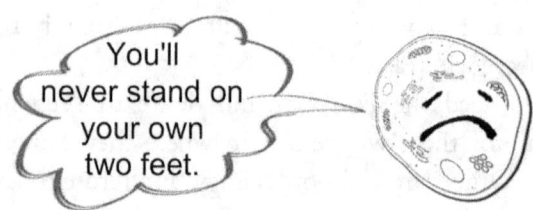

WE DISENTANGLED ALL THE NEGATIVE WORDS, THOUGHTS, and energies snarled around each toe. It took months to unravel and free up each of Emily's toes; we accomplished something the mainstream medical profession could not touch. As we lovingly unbound Emily's toes, she could stand her ground, take a stance on her own two feet, and radically change her life. After completing our sessions, Emily got a job, moved to her own apartment, and started a relationship.

Thoughts from our great grandparents and words of our parents, hiding, lurking below the surface, thriving in the unconscious, influence our lives. Carrying and upholding beliefs can be hard work. Some opinions are so old and ingrained that they get heavy; centuries of dust and grime add to the burden.

Some beliefs encrusted with Bottom Sludge and Nasties can be challenging to uncover. You probably have had the experience that no matter how much you talk to someone about something, they just don't get it. Their neural programming will not allow them to see a different perspective. Beliefs are ingrained into neural programs, wired into how the synapses in our brains fire. It's profound to watch the brain bypass higher reasoning and jump directly to firmly held beliefs. Unfortunately, many people don't want to change; they are devoted to upholding the Fear Bot as the defender of truth.

Thoughts hang on to the belief's internal structure. Like a coat rack, opinions add evidence to the truth of your premises. Ideas come in all shapes and sizes, like a closet filled with old stuff you've forgotten you owned. But who and where did these thoughts originate?

One set of core beliefs is victim consciousness. Victim consciousness is the disconnection from your soul essence, the essential self of who you are. Victim consciousness feels like a pit in your stomach, the sinking feeling, shrinking into your small self, feeling powerless. Others are to blame. It's their fault they made you feel this way. Mental fog, you don't know what to do, can't see your way out, and want to give up.

The old thoughts yell, "If you let go of being a victim, you're not loyal to the Fear Bot." We feel obligated to act like a victim; our friends and family will be mad if we let it go. It's like being ostracized for leaving a cult.

Invite your body to let go of the burden of carrying the illusion in your thoughts and beliefs. It's a life crusher, soul-sucking killer to take on the fabricated load of the Fear Bot. So, give your thoughts permission to leave—the freedom to evolve into something new, fresh, and extraordinary.

Many people claim that thoughts create reality; as your thought forms transform, your reality changes.

Neural Programs

You might have moments when you realize you're acting exactly like your mother or father, even though it's the last thing you want to do. This is because when you were tiny, your nervous system imprinted off your parents and the people around you.

So over time, we take on their good and not-so-positive qualities, actions, mannerisms, speech, and neural programs. We take on the drama of being messed up, crazy, and fraught with worry. We forget we can shift our roles by transforming our neural programs.

The neurobiologist Dr. Carla Shatz states that neurons that fire together wire together.[5] So every time the pattern triggers, more nerve bundles weave together, and the problem grows.

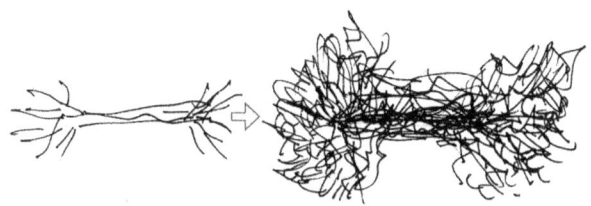

Triggering any part of the neural network sets off a chain reaction throughout the whole body. For example, in the illustration below, a headache occurs, and vision shuts down in fear. Afraid to speak up, shallow breathing, solar plexus constricts, guts churn, genitals clamp shut. Sometimes we can track the external trigger. Other times random events trigger the process.

Trauma, stress, and accidents influence your neural programs. Some neural programs are passed down in your lineage; others build up over time. Still, others function in the unconscious, impacting your life beyond your consciousness. Several neural programs create unhealthy habits. Unfortunately, changing the routine is arduous and usually doesn't stick.

Your wiring was hacked when you were little; your essence was pirated and used to run the Fear Bot. The only one who can change your code and programming is you.

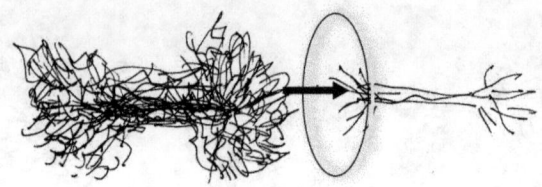

Strand by strand, unravel the neural bundles. Change the neural Fear Bot, connect to your Soul Circuitry, and then fundamental transformation happens; watch your well-being, happiness, and inner delight expand. As your neurology shifts, reality changes.

Implants and Brain Clamps

Another way the Fear Bot functions is through external apparatus wired in your body to keep you thinking and behaving in specific, prescribed routes.

For example, you may have a looping tape player repeating messages from early childhood about how bad, unworthy, or unlovable you are.

The inner critic's incessant blah, blah, continues, nagging, criticizing, and making you wrong.

Some implants are in your head and manipulate your vision and mental processes to see the world through a particular lens. As a result, a narrow focus and tunnel vision rule, while new perspectives and possibilities don't exist.

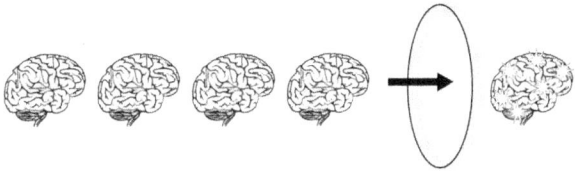

Imagine a transparent plastic model of a brain squished on top of your brain. The plastic brain cap is like invisible braces or a plastic retainer with a wire to straighten your teeth but covers the gray matter in your brain.

Over time, your brain's neuroplasticity conforms to all the curves and crevices of the enforced device. The convoluted plastic clamp on the brain distorts perceptions and only allows seeing and thinking in specific ways. Forced thinking through rigid pathways, only certain brain parts connect with others, and particular neural impulses fire in a fixed sequence. Free thought is inhibited; the device ensures your mentality conforms to the prescribed worldview.

We are bombarded daily with the news, advertising, TV, and propaganda about how to think and see the world. Messaging over time programs what we believe is the truth. Hence, the system trains how the brain functions and what neurons connect to create a specific worldview.

The good news is that you can change how our brains function. In *The Brain that Changes Itself,* Dr. Norman Doidge notes numerous case studies of the brain's neuroplasticity and evidence that thoughts change the structures and functions of our brains.[6]

Now imagine you can take the plastic tray off your brain. Slowly, gently, bit by bit, it starts to dissolve. Love is the solvent that eats away the enforced slavery in our brain's neural pathways.

Incredible freedom arises as you take the implants and energetic cap off your brain and allow your brain function to follow your soul essence rather than external programming and manipulation. Your body's natural intelligence and brilliance direct your brain functioning rather than mind manipulation and external coercion. New neural connections spark insights, revelations, and a profound new way to see the world emerges.

The Matrix

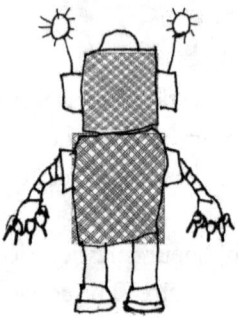

Years ago, I had a captivating dream, one of those deep-seated dreams that creates an impact and stays with you. In this dream, many people are in a gas chamber, names written in a giant ledger book with a red line down the side. The tops of our heads are screwed into a large grid hanging low from the ceiling—wired in, programmed to think in specific ways and act according to a prescribed plan.

Lined up in neat, straight rows, sitting on rickety slate brown metal folding chairs, a docile woman sits at the front of the room, watching over the group. It is time for extinction, yet there is no reason for anyone to die. I ask why we are there and why we can't cross off our names and leave. The woman in charge doesn't know why we can't do it but has never heard of such a thing.

The Inner (R)Evolution:

I unfasten the screw connecting my head to the grid and walk out. I find the book and start crossing out all the names. While waiting for everyone to walk out, only one woman joins me. All the others sat there with their heads screwed into the grid, complacent, following orders passed down from above.

Twenty years later, the dream takes on a more profound significance. The matrix is more complex than the dream indicates. Different matrix forms inhabit all twelve dimensions, appearing as obstacles, blocks, and challenges, telling us what to do, sending conflicting messages, and triggering opposing neural programs.

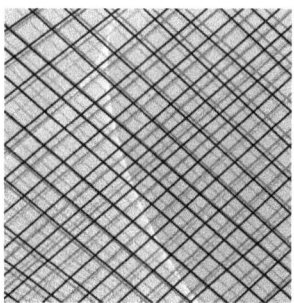

The matrix is an energetic rigid structure of reality, broken down into tiny cubicles that create feeling alone, separate, unworthy, unloved, and not good enough. The individual boxes make you feel incomplete, searching outside yourself for wholeness and fulfillment.

The multi-layered grid structure compartmentalizes beliefs and experiences. For example, the message in one cubicle is that your body needs to look a certain way for you to be loved. Another box holds the statement that you are unworthy of love. Yet another pigeonhole says that if you stuff your needs, you'll be loved. The matrix enhances inner torment and negates your brilliance.

We live in the matrix, in place from childhood, passed through the lineage, which yields a particular worldview. Like the quilt of life, the childhood blanket we revert to when scared. A delicate process, gossamer threads woven together for millennia create a subtle, substantial, firm background. Insidious, sneaky, lurking in the shadows, ducking around corners, the matrix ensures a perspective filled with fear, disease, and torment.

Survival kicks in, we try to escape, but we can't find the way out. Alcohol, food, drugs, prescriptions, shopping, cigarettes, and sex create a momentary escape, followed by a crash into the current reality.

The good news is there's an escape route; dive deep inside, past the fears, blocks, resistance, and panic. Connect to your Soul Circuitry, and the narrow vision, boxed in manipulated ways of seeing reality, begins to shift.

Each dimension has its lies and propaganda, trying to cut you down, squish you, and keep you boxed in. For example, the matrix in the 3rd dimension is related to self-hatred and self-loathing. The matrix on the 6th dimension is about believing in external authority instead of trusting your inner knowing.

One by one, climb out of the matrices and escape the inner torment. Every time you release one of the Matrices, notice how your inner landscape transforms. Evaporating each matrix creates more abundant joy, inner freedom, and pleasure to savor this magnificent life. We are creating more space for you, your brilliance, and your vision.

VEILS OF ILLUSION

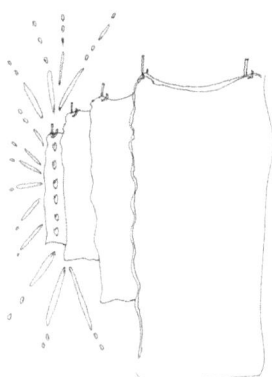

As you clear out the mechanisms of the Fear Bot and gain more clarity, you start bumping into the edge of the Fear Bot reality and the Veils of Illusion. In the movie, The Truman Show, Truman discovers the edge of his made-up reality. He finds the guys behind the scenes with the machines manipulating the environment. The same happens with humanity; we live in a projected worldview that controls thoughts through the news and provokes emotions with manufactured world events.

An image builds up over the ages creating an overlay or cloak over humanity. The hype keeps growing, with more smokescreens of fake news and censorship on mainstream and social media. Now, it's harder to sift out the truth.

Bumping up against the Veils of Illusion can be scary. The distorted, twisted reality and the depths of human torture and slavery are astonishing. The current reality's lies, deception, and propaganda fabricate the Veils of Illusion, like movie sets or the background in a virtual reality game—a false backdrop formed by the Fear Bot model.

Sometimes as the Veils of Illusion collapse, doubts and old inner programs surface. Imagine a net holding a layer of the Fear Bot. As the net drops, everything it retained, comes to the surface to be cleared away. It's like removing a thick yucky quilt covering a window in the attic to find a dirty window filled with cobwebs and layers of dirt. Clean the window and see a spectacular view and a fresh perspective.

Peek behind the Veils of Illusion, expose the current paradigm underbelly, and discover how our neural processes create reality. Unveil the forbidden, behind-the-scenes manipulation that makes up modern society. Surprising insights arise. The dots connect. The light switches on.

Many spiritual texts state that this is all an illusion, but that's hard to grasp. We sit on chairs, and we eat food; everything seems tangible. The illusion is the picture of reality. You produce your vision of truth, world-view, and life. But there's no freedom. You are generating responses to mechanisms in your body and outer reality that manipulate you to react a certain way.

At times the Veils of Illusion look like a blank wall. Mental fog takes over; we're unable to see a clear direction. Exhaustion creeps in; we're too tired to think, so we want to retreat into the known way. Other times the curtain is full of distractions to keep us preoccupied.

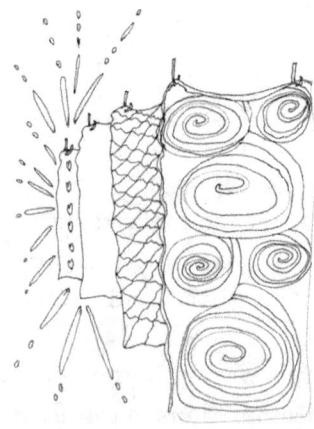

Each dimension has different veils to prevent us from seeing the greater depths of reality; blinders keep us repeating the same patterns of the past, thinking and believing brainwashed ideals and perpetuating the current distorted existence.

Start to notice where the Veils of Illusion are beginning to drop. Get curious when you read or hear something; how does it make you feel? Do you feel open and expansive, filled with love, or covered with a dark blanket of fear where you want to curl up and hide? What happens when you examine the thought or belief? Is it covered in Nasties, Bottom Sludge, wired in your nervous system from your parents, or some unknown source? Or do you see a new perspective, gain clarity, and things start to make more profound sense?

Trauma

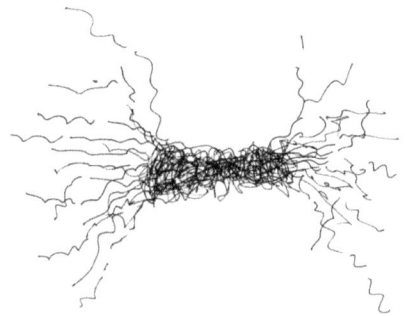

Embedded trauma is another aspect of the Fear Bot. Trauma is what happened to you; it's not who you are. It's a response to the past and gets triggered until it transforms. Underneath the trauma is a healthy person who wants self-expression.

It's surprising to discover how trauma eats up life force, vitality, and brilliance. Trauma is overwhelming situations, adverse events, or the shock of an accident. Trauma is when the life force energy stops, stuck in time, encased in the past. A fragmentation occurs, disconnection from your Soul Self, and the part becomes numb. Your essence is left behind; fear keeps replaying over and over. Trauma keeps you rooted in survival and fear.

Collective trauma builds with each generation, war, drought, famine, and epidemics. The global wounding, stories of pain, shock, and suffering gather in the collective unconscious. And now, humanity has reached a state of global trauma with the pandemic. As a result, we overreact or can't feel—isolated, separate, lost connections, and an inner fracture between mind, body, and soul.

Trauma also leads to addiction, alcohol, drugs, prescriptions, sex, food, adventure, and work. Anything to escape the inner torment and torture that eats our bones devours the soul and sucks up life-source energy. The trauma pattern keeps looping until we change it.

Addiction is also a response to trauma. People aren't addicts; they are traumatized. Calling someone an addict spreads a lie, imposes more layers of self-hatred, and perpetuates the trauma.

"I'm an alcoholic, an addict." You're not an addict. Your body is so brilliant that it doesn't respond well to toxins and alcohol. Your cells listen and react whenever you or someone else tells you you're an addict and alcoholic. It's all a trauma response.

The words addiction and addict elicit a gruesome image. Skid Row, sleeping on the street, a needle hangs off pale flesh—a bottle of booze in a brown paper bag. The word addiction evokes hidden panic that keeps the cycle going. Saying "I am an addict" commands the cells and neurons to perform addictive behavior every time we say those words.

Trauma is like a multi-tendril beast from a gruesome fairytale. It invades all dimensions, trying to gain a stronghold on your body. It grows every time the trauma is triggered; more nerve bundles join the Fear Bot. As the activated nerves send out messages of fear and worthlessness, they keep reaching further, hungry, devouring more of your soul essence, spiraling downwards, hopelessness, and depression set in.

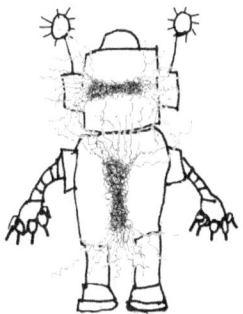

Goblins of the past haunt the night; anxiety rules the day. We search inside, trying to discover what's wrong. "How did I fail? What did I do that was so bad to make me feel this crappy inside?" It's a complicated web, held together with childhood programming, fed with the collective unconscious; each dimension contains various dysfunctional neural programs and patterns. It's impressive that humanity functions as well as it does.

We begin to believe that the beast is who we are. It gets so awful we don't even want to look. We know we're bad inside; we've been told that throughout our life. Shrunken and defeated, we keep ourselves small. Why bother? My life doesn't matter anymore.

Part of your body disconnects, and a deep fear of survival takes over. You become a stone; life force energy cut off—over time, disease develops, perceived as aches and pains to be drugged, cut out, medicated. Then there's the merry-go-round of drugs and medications, diminishing the symptoms while still feeding the beast.

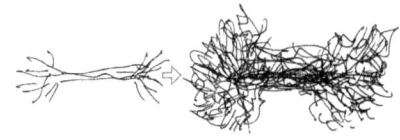

No matter how much you try to control yourself, the old wiring is still there and gets triggered. That's why people go back to smoking, drinking, and binging.

The Nasties want to ensure the pattern continues to trigger so they can eat and thrive on our life force energy. So they stir up a ruckus in your body, sirens scream, flashing lights, and road blockades keep you from progressing. The message is if you move on, you will die. When you evolve, the Nasties starve and die, not your essence.

You watch it happening, repeating the same thing over and over, but it's the Fear Bot firing your neurology. It's hiding in the unconscious, beyond your control. You can see yourself careening, quickly accelerating, feeling powerless, spinning down the dark tunnel of self-destruction.

When you realize the trauma is not the truth of who you are, you can imagine corrupt neural programs and a bunch of Nasties trying to scare you. Then, it's easier to take control and transform the Fear Bot running your life.

Trauma is not cleared by yanking out, sedating with toxic prescriptions, or cajoling with talk. Sugar and drugs keep the trauma in place, feed the wound, and keep the cycle going. The greatest love, tenderness, gratitude, and pleasure release trauma. Following joy and pleasure, a curved pathway is a key to healing wounds.

Safety in your tissues, muscles, and nerves releases the trauma. Trauma is stuck energy that wants to flow out of your body. Some of it is so old and embedded we don't question it. We assume that's how life is. It's always been that way. We tend to believe these old-known patterns rather than challenge our ability to create radical inner transformation.

It's time to release the heavy burdens and give the fear, anger, and sadness their freedom. A radical idea, to let go and give your trauma freedom. In the process, the old energy shifts into a higher frequency. You can't take trauma with you as you evolve. The trauma needs to be left behind; it doesn't fit into the newer, ever-evolving version of who you are.

The trauma has carved down deep, creating vast pits. Your wounds are the gateway to your greatness and freedom. As the anguish clears, there's space for your soul essence to fill and reside.

Tiny pools of your soul essence gather together, casting a network throughout your body. As minuscule reservoirs of wisdom link with this unseen new neural network, the depth of your experience radiates.

Your body rewires, and new interconnections form, leading to unique insights, deep awe, and delicious pleasure. Profound wisdom, new solutions, and brilliant visions take hold. Your body and soul merge with your mental capacities to share your mystical inner knowing from the depth of your experience.

My Trauma

It feels like I've been at war with my trauma since childhood. And when I got older, more educated, and started seeing the trauma, it felt like the battle ramped up. Like I have to deal with, eradicate, and annihilate my trauma. Sometimes I wanted to bomb out my trauma, but that would create an enormous hole.

I moved eighty-seven times, trying to escape the bomb. I knew what was happening; I didn't know how to transform the trauma pattern. For years, I packed boxes, hauled furniture, drove a 20-foot U-Haul truck, towed my car across the country, searched for safety, and tried to find a home. Storage units sprinkled through various States. Always on the run, moving to a new place where I know no one. Pack, move, unpack, repeat and repeat. For decades, I was on guard, waiting for the attack, the next bomb to drop.

I've lived in five countries, traveled around the world about six times, and had gazillions of road trips and solo adventures into the deep wilderness. I sometimes felt like I would explode if I stayed in one place for too long. Perpetual motion infused with times of collapse. It's hard to bomb a moving target.

I knew I had been trying to outrun the bomb for years, but the knowledge wasn't enough. I needed to discover how to heal the trauma and rewire my nervous system so that I felt safe. No place on earth felt safe; I could be annihilated in an instant. If I disagreed and challenged patriarchy, I could be blown to bits. That's the information wired in my body. From my pre-birth onward, my dad was the top engineer building the United States' nuclear warfare, the world's impressive weapons of mass destruction.

As a child, if you had a violent parent, you knew how to pick up the cues and when to hide. You could feel the frequency of violence and rage emanating from your parents. I could feel the bomb frequencies radiating from my dad whenever he came home after watching bombs explode. Like every kid, we soak up what's in our environment. The wound was so deep nothing could touch it. How do I heal the gaping energetic hole created by the 131 nuclear explosions my father energetically brought home?

Bomb stock, that's what my ex-husband used to call me. I blew up toasters, vacuum cleaners, and washing machines just by turning them on. I used my trusty craft soldering iron to reconnect the frayed wires. One day, feeling particularly crappy, I turned on my Apple computer, the original model that looked like a giant bug. As I directed my finger to the start button, I watched a bolt of neon green energy shoot out my finger. The zapped tubes crackled, sparks flew, smoke billowed, scorched burnt wires smelled putrid. The repairman insisted that lightning had struck my computer.

How can my body operate properly with shockwave frequencies of nuclear explosions imprinted in my nervous system? Deep trauma cuts off the body's functioning like a shiny, silver kitchen knife cleaver chopping through a thick chunk of bloody red meat. One sharp blow severs the entire slab. The same thing happens with the neural patterns in our bodies. Imagine energetically chopping through those connecting neurons. Trauma is like being stuck between layers of glass; the cells and neurons can't communicate with each other. They don't know how to find each other again.

What happens if I love and honor my trauma? All those things I've lived through are forbidden to discuss. For years all I could do was thank one specific part. The whole glob of trauma was much too large; it infiltrated every cell in my body. Every neuron and fiber of my being has been traumatized to the core.

My DNA is from one egg and one sperm covered in weapons-grade radiation. The depth of destructive hate-filled energy has influenced every breath of my life. When I started seeing and feeling that, I felt so separate, isolated, and alone. How could anybody possibly love me? I was despicable to my core.

A weird arrogance; I'm more traumatized than you. Years ago, my sister and I used to do this on the phone, to see who could come up with the worst story, the most victimized, the deepest sufferings, and the greatest devastation. I stopped playing the game; she wanted to continue. I discovered gratitude, and it worked. I wanted to share my excitement and joy with her, but she was committed to the victim role.

Trauma brings up so much resistance; it's a disconnection from source. I'm a vegetable, limp, withering on the couch—the trauma response takes over all rational thought, so I can't function. The block of trauma that had tendrils connecting to every cell is dissolving. My reality is dying. I feel lost. Panic attacks ignite, and pain screams. Everything known is dissolving; tears flow, rage surges. I'm exhausted.

What part dies, and what remains? Which previous selves are ready to move on? Childhood traumas set free. Everything that has kept me in the patriarchal mindset reality bubble is dying. All the shoulds, have to's, and self-judgments want to flee. The container of my life, beliefs, and thoughts are up for grabs.

And now, a new awakening is occurring.

My trauma is mine. I can do what I want with it. Instead of trauma being a nasty thing in my body, sucking my guts, I've changed my mind. My trauma has made me strong and taught me how to rise up and survive against all odds. Instead of feeling deflated, defective, and inferior by my trauma, what if it's a powerhouse to assist my evolution? I changed my inner brainwashing into radical self-acceptance and love.

A new opening is happening. I'm sinking into me as I invite the fireball of my trauma to be fully loved. Inner streaming, the trauma block swirls and develops into a waterfall. Tiny drops, bubbles release and become little dots rearranging, creating new energetic, iridescent, luminescent, shimmering DNA.

My whole body seems different. Each cell feels healthier, more alive, and rooted in safety and joy. Trauma was the fuel, the fire, behind my massive creativity. I'm curious to see what will evolve.

Waves circle back and forth, pulsating, growing. The old traumatized cells now dance, sliding in inner harmony instead of clamped down. The internal orchestration between the masculine and the feminine, the upper and lower parts of my body, reaches the next level of delightful enjoyment.

More of my multidimensional Soul Self fills the spaces left by the fleeing trauma. My next level of embodiment, more of me is present on earth, the tormented spaces now filled with contentment, satisfaction, and profound freedom.

Pleasure surges, joy expands; I'm dancing in the sunlight.

The Inner (R)Evolution:

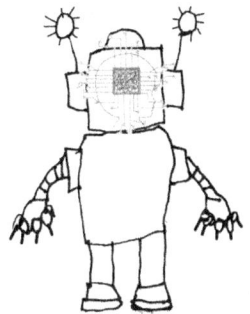

Sometimes it seems easier to pretend the Fear Bot doesn't exist and live a half-baked life than to journey into the unknown with bravery.

Not Enough

*I'm not enough
and I refuse to believe that
I can change
it's evident that
my life won't transform
and it's foolish to presume that
I create my luscious reality*

- Dr. Cynthia Miller

Are you ready to untwist your perceived reality and open up to a more expansive, powerful version of who you are?

*I create my luscious reality
and it's foolish to presume that
my life won't transform
it's evident that
I can change
and I refuse to believe that
I'm not enough*

Release all the Fear Bots that say that you aren't enough. It takes great courage and guts to see the depth of distortion and cruelty lurking within. But, once cleared, your life takes on a new depth of inner harmony and joyous delight. Know, love, and trust yourself – the relationship with yourself determines everything in your life.

The Fear Bot runs the world and is inside your body. The Fear Bot knows every possible way to sabotage your life. For your physical 3-D form to house all of who you are, you have to kick out the Fear Bot to make the space. But, once lovingly dissolved, the energies morph into delicious support.

You can control the fear dial in your body, and you have the power to clear the Fear Bot out of your body. Your body is yours; learn how to take control. It's time to evolve beyond the clutching grasp of anxiety and domination. Read on to discover how to use the Trailblazers Technologies to unlock your energy, power, and freedom.

4. TRAILBLAZER TECHNOLOGIES AND SOUL CIRCUITRY

To move from your current state into your Soul Circuitry and brilliant flowing multidimensional soul, use the proven, time-tested Trailblazer Technologies. Uncomplicated and accessible, these tools are easy to use—to unleash humanity from the Fear Bot shackles and mind manipulation that keep us small and confined. These deceptively simple healing tools are helpful in every dimension and permanently dismantle all parts of the Fear Bot.

The journey is releasing the layers of fear to uncover and expose who you are. A messy process, pulling back, the oozing, festering infected bandages covering gaping, sore wounds. The Trailblazer Technologies are the cleanup crew, kicking out the Fear Bot and loving you back to wholeness. Trailblazer Technologies are energetic tools to create magic in your life and the world. They work best when you come from a place of innocent, grateful curiosity and joy.

THE TRAILBLAZER TECHNOLOGIES INCLUDE:
- Healing Angels
- Spirals of Love and Gratitude
- Secret Flow
- Light Codes
- The Language of the Cells, the Language of the Soul
- Soul Frequency

DANCING LIGHT CODES, FLUTTERING ANGEL WINGS, AND swirling spirals are some of the wondrous Trailblazer Technologies. On the surface, they may seem flighty, whimsical, or woo-woo to transform the Fear Bot. These proven, time-tested evolutionary technologies have assisted thousands of my clients who had very different goals and healing paths. Each technology is a multidimensional tool that works deeply in us because we are connected to source. Play with the Trailblazer Technologies and discover mysteries inside that lead to your freedom.

SOUL CIRCUITRY

Soul Circuitry

Your unique Soul Circuitry is the very architecture of who and what you are. Your Soul Circuitry is the fundamental spiritual and energetic framework for transforming your consciousness and life. The Merriam-Webster dictionary defines the soul as the immaterial essence, animating principle, or actuating cause of an individual life, a person's total self. Another way to understand soul is a *continuum* of your divine light or being.

Your Soul Circuitry is a spinning, luminescent, holographic, toroidal energy field. It replaces and is the complete bio-spiritual evolution of the tangled-up Childhood Circuitry. It is the energetic framework for merging body and soul and remembering who you are. It's a safe home in all dimensions, a place to heal and regenerate. Soul Circuitry, built to the blueprint of your soul, is alive, fluid, and expands to incorporate all of who you are.

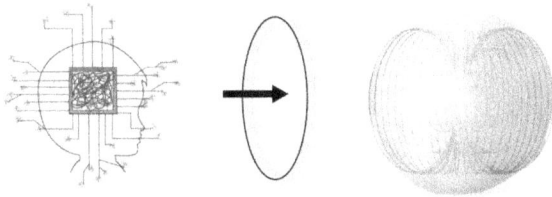

You inherited your Childhood Circuitry from your parents' genetic and epigenetic memory. The Childhood Circuitry pulls you back into the past or the anxiety of the future. It can be really helpful to understand how deep your Childhood Circuitry goes. The Childhood Circuitry is the foundation to what's underneath what you think, how you emotionally react, and why you're stuck in seeing yourself and others in the same way year after year. To transform our Childhood Circuitry, which takes time, the ingrained, ancient responses wired into you from the past are no longer triggered.

In the Soul Circuitry, you are in the present, as your soul essence frequency leads the way, rather than the collective unconsciousness, childhood trauma, or negative karma.

Instead of trying to jam yourself into a reality that doesn't fit or where large chunks of you are made wrong or shoved aside, choose your Soul Circuitry.

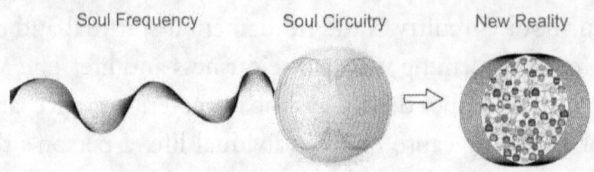

Detaching from your Childhood Circuitry is a profoundly courageous act. You've relied on your Childhood Circuitry your entire life, and unplugging it creates new cellular openings to welcome lost aspects from your past to return home to you. It goes back even further than the start of this life... long missing soul fragments, gone for millennia, return to a fantastic welcoming of your own sacred body. When you feel ready, invite back in parts of yourself beyond 3-D reality, bringing in knowledge from far-off galaxies.

Remember, we are exploring the magical path laid out for you by your soul, the pathway of joy, deep play, and genuine fun that leads to living your deepest heart's desires. There is complete space and permission for the expanded, more incredible version of you, at each step of your becoming your own Soul Circuitry. Your soul essence is in charge, guiding your journey. You are Home, in yourself, comfortable in your skin, at ease in your thoughts, and ready to explore the unknown.

HEALING ANGELS

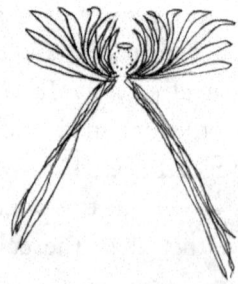

Lifelong best friends, the angels are an integral, intimate part of my reality. My cohorts for decades, I started flying with the angels in my dreams when I was two. That was in 1948. We've worked together with clients for decades; miraculous healings occurred.

Forty years of clinical practice working with thousands of people, quantum physics, and gut-wrenching personal experience are the basis for this time-tested and proven Trailblazer Technology.

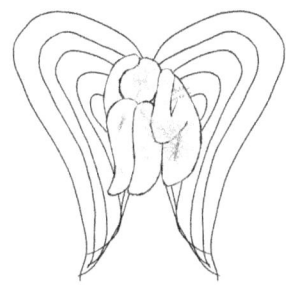

Imagine the Healing Angels holding your wounded inner child. Wrapped in massive, mighty soft angel wings, protected and safe, your inner child relaxes into comfort, compassion, and love. Old trauma dissolves. It's safe to be vulnerable and open as you invite the Bottom Sludge and old programs to leave—your nervous system recalibrates to the frequencies of love and safety rather than fear and terror.

Along with being held in safety, tiny angel wings sweep out the rotting debris, cobwebs, oozing pus, and scars. Your soul emerges as your Childhood Circuitry releases the pain, scared, traumatized, neglected parts. Angels sprinkle love, and glistening light sparkles throughout your cells. Joy bubbles up from crusty old spaces now filled with love. Luscious freedom to be you fills your body.

The angels have your back and keep you safe and protected, a 9th dimension technology available to all. Anyone can call on the Healing Angels; you have direct access, and no intermediary is required. A renegade group of angels, unconnected to religion, doctrine, or belief; instead, they are dedicated to humanity's evolution, joy, and delight.

Available to everyone, call on the Healing Angels with gratitude, an open heart, and a willingness to let go of your old thoughts and hurts. Don't approach them demanding or begging on your knees. Instead, invite them in as your dearest friend, someone you love and trust deeply.

The Healing Angels are magical beings that respond to your love and gratitude. They enjoy being of service and delight in assisting you to wake up to your inner magnificence.

The angels will assist you to release all aspects of the Fear Bot. For me, they are most effective in clearing trauma, rewiring neural programs, and cleaning toxic corrupt DNA codes. You will discover what works best for you as you work with your Healing Angels.

The Housing Angels

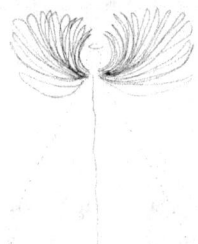

Sometimes, it's appropriate to move, find a new home, change the scenery, and shift your environment as you evolve. Invite the housing angels to be of assistance to help you.

Be open and on the lookout for hidden messages, flashes of insight, and an inner nudge. It's not a logical, linear process; finding your new home is like following the breadcrumbs, trusting the path will lead you to your next magical home for your evolution.

Get to know your angels. Their sizes range from minuscule to larger than earth; their wings have incredible shapes, iridescent, luminous colors, and textures like feathers and billowing clouds. Waiting in the wings, ready to be of service, they only come when invited.

The Inner (R)Evolution:

Discover the magic, play, and delight the angels' love to share, sprinkling light sparkles throughout your body and the cosmos. Start by inviting the angels to assist in clearing Bottom Sludge and then expand into clearing corrupt DNA codes. Have fun and detect the mysterious ways the healing angels assist in your inner evolution.

Spiraling Radical Gratitude and Love

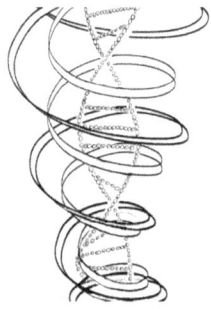

The high frequency of Spirals of Love and Gratitude dissolves the Nasties that guard and keep our treasures safely hidden. Thank the demons lurking in the unconscious; set them free.

Imagine Nasties taunting you, saying what you are working on is worthless, you will never succeed, and you don't matter. See huge spirals of love and Gratitude surrounding you and the Nasties. The vortex spins faster, like a hurricane, dissolving the low frequencies in its path.

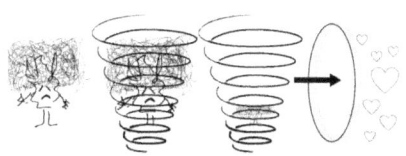

When told, "I love you," the shocked Nasties don't know how to respond. They've never heard those words before. The Nasties melt in Gratitude and love like Day of the Dead sugar skulls; the fear dies when exposed to Spirals of Love and Gratitude exposing the magical gifts that reside within.

On your journey of awakening and remembering who you are, Gratitude is simple, profound, and powerful. But, unfortunately, it's easy to overlook Gratitude because it's so uncomplicated.

Radical Gratitude is not some wimpy practice; extreme Gratitude is giving thanks for the good, the bad, and the unacceptable. It's hard to determine what's yours and everyone else's since it was all programmed before your mind could discern—Spirals of Gratitude sorts out the inner jumbled-up mess. Getting down in the nitty-gritty, facing the terror and horrors in your body, is where the actual practice resides.

Gratitude dissolves the Nasties that trigger fear, anger, and pain in our bodies. Gratitude transforms neural patterns, programs, DNA, and the Bottom Sludge while accentuating the higher frequencies of love and joy.

It's so satisfying, rewarding, and enriching to watch the Nasties that have been taunting you for years waste away in Spirals of Love, like watching a ghost expire in flames.

Allow yourself to delight in the demise of all the negative talk that led you astray. Relish the devouring; the Nastie was living off your precious life juice. Now you have more energy for yourself and more pleasure to enjoy your life and create your dreams. But, of course, people connected to the Fear Bot will call it blasphemy; they want to keep you small, so you'll continue to do their dirty work while they rise to the top.

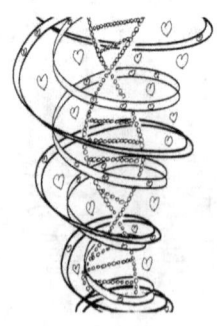

Rather than wage war on your wounds, give thanks to your inner trauma. Embedded in the past are the seeds of greatness, the roots of change, and the new paradigm. So, dive deep within and find the gift that is hiding buried, your internal treasures.

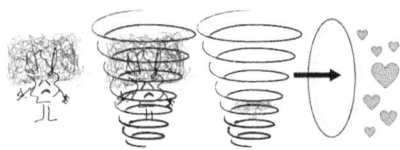

Get cozy in bed or on the couch under your favorite blanket. Support your spine with pillows. Close your eyes, take a deep breath, and relax. Imagine Gratitude spiraling around your body, creating a cocoon of safety. Now envision Spirals of Gratitude, like corkscrews, burrowing through the pain, wounds, and hurt. Surround the Nasties with Gratitude and love and watch them melt. Keep going until you burst into light and joy, deep enough so your cells experience bliss. The Fear Bot leaves bit by bit, and your soul fills those carved-out spaces in your body. Thank the fear for going in so deep that it created a tunnel headed toward your soul's heart. Chapter 10, The Process, outlines a detailed step-by-step process.

Gratitude opens new vistas in your brain and body, happiness beyond everyday experience, unlocking the wellspring of joy and the frequency of delight. For radical transformation, the key is to use it properly. You can use forgiveness, compassion, or any high frequency. But for more profound results, make sure it's spiraling; everything in nature is moving; atoms and galaxies are spinning.

Spiraling Gratitude and Love takes you from victim to self-mastery, from blame to self-responsibility, from being run by your unconscious to conscious proficiency, to transforming the world of war, fear, and terror into a world of cooperation, peace, and Gratitude. You can change all the parts you want to destroy and hate through love. A mind-shifting approach that goes against everything you were taught.

For deeper insights, my book, *The Art of Radical Gratitude*[1], explores how gratitude spirals transform consciousness. Photos illuminate the details of the simple yet profound alchemical process of transforming fear into love.

Secret Flow

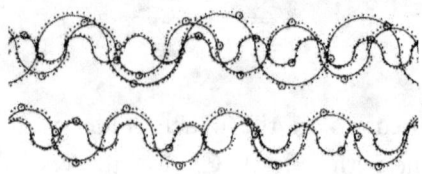

Secret Flow, a 12th dimension technology, is the highest frequency of each dimension, with brilliant wisdom, miracles, and healing energies. A joyful essence, filled with sparkling light and pleasure, Secret Flow meanders into long-hidden, dried-up, starving nooks and crannies, bringing life force, renewing, regenerating frequencies.

When you encounter crusty Bottom Sludge, picture thick chunks of glop, dried, hardened, and more sludge piled on for generations. Compacted for eons, rock hard holds the most profound secrets. Now envision the high frequencies of Secret Flow, breaking up, dissolving the goop—the solidified trauma energies released, cascading through your body.

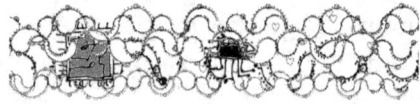

Imagine that Secret Flow is a flowing gel that captures hidden junk and washes it out of your energy field. Like a magical river, Secret Flow clears the slime around DNA. Or a crystal-clear waterfall, washing away the self-hatred, dredge, and mental chatter.

Invite your Secret Flow to undulate, slide, hydrate and nourish every cell. Feel the channels of your soul essence open; exquisite delight pours,

The Inner (R)Evolution:

gliding through you. Secret Flow trickles down from the head, cascading through the heart, into the pelvic bowl, and overflows. Toes wiggle in delight. Heart opens. Happiness abounds; joy bubbles up, deliciously alive, here on earth, in your body—safe, innocent, ready to play, designing a new reality. Expansive openings occur, mysteries uncovered, and hidden gifts revealed.

You've had moments of being in the flow, connected, alive, full of clarity, passion, and pleasure. That's Secret Flow, a companion of your Soul Circuitry swirling through all of you.

Light Codes

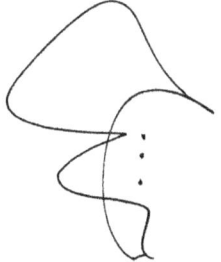

Light Codes are streams of luminescent, iridescent energy filled with love and transformational frequencies. Light Codes, a 7th dimension technology, transmute the old and make way for the new. Like a snowflake, each is unique, delivering packets of encoded awakening.

Light Codes merge symbols and light energies, similar to angels, devas, elementals, and nature spirits. Alive, Light Codes are a magical part of claiming the reality of who you are.

Alphabets like water, each character, symbol, and transmitted energy packet are ever-changing. Light codes dance, not confined to the page like pen and ink, but remain fixed to the human eye.

Light Codes, unknown to the rational mind, flow with joy. This is because light language connects to the soul rather than the logical mind. As a result, Light Codes bring the most profound pleasure, filled with Gratitude, love, and childlike delight. When you open up to receive and decode Light Codes on each dimension from your multidimensional selves, incredible magic and mystery unfolds.

There are two ways to use Light Codes, drawing and imagining. Drawing Light Codes is like your handwriting; they contain your unique frequency.

Let your creativity flow. Take a piece of paper, invite in the Light Codes, relax, and start to draw. Sometimes it's easier if you begin with your non-dominant hand. Try writing from right to left instead of writing from left to right. Your drawings won't look like mine; they contain your soul essence. Keep doodling and inviting in your soul frequency. When creating Light Codes, my body fills with joy, a smile beams, and happiness abounds.

The second way to use Light Codes is to imagine these invisible light packets spiraling through your body. Light Codes activate information and wisdom carried in your DNA. Your body resonates with specific light-encoded data, which shifts the consciousness of your cellular structures. Thus, light language is a way to communicate in each dimension.

The Inner (R)Evolution:

Twelve Dimensions of Light Codes

Each dimension has unique Light Codes, filled with awakening, healing, and love. The luminescent high-frequency transmission involving light, color, sound, and sacred geometry clears through the dense 3-D fear, igniting joy and pleasure. Light Codes help clear out the Bottom Sludge, unconscious programs and dissolve the matrix. Like Pac-Man, magical packets of information, Light Codes consume the old toxic waste and dissolve the karmic glue holding the encoded neural programming.

INVITE THE LIGHT CODES TO TRANSFORM YOUR CHILDHOOD Circuitry, creating space for your Soul Circuitry to emerge. Emissaries of awakening, sprinkle Light Codes throughout your day. Daily doses help dissolve the fear-driven, panic-ridden energies that believe you aren't good enough, don't amount to anything, or are unlovable.

Light Codes are ready to serve your evolutionary process. They bring in high-frequency information necessary for your evolution and transformation. As a result, Light Codes are a fabulous adjunct to your Trailblazer Technologies toolkit.

THE LANGUAGES OF YOUR CELLS AND SOUL

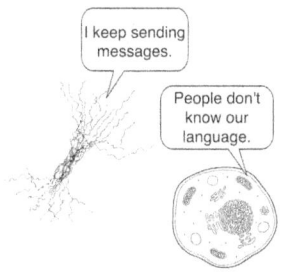

Your cells are talking about you. What are they saying? All parts of your body are in contact, but we've cut off our consciousness from our cells. So, it's hard to understand the language of our cells, the words of our nervous system, and the requests of our body. Working with the languages of your cells and soul is a 5th dimension technology.

The incessant babble of the Fear Bot, self-doubt, and worry interfere with the cell's communication. The messages of unworthiness, being unloved, and abandonment jumble up the internal communication pathways. In trauma, the communication keeps looping in the past, unable to connect to the present.

How much dis-ease is caused by the messages and directions your cells receive from unconscious chatter filled with negativity and fear? Your aches and pains are trying to get your attention; they want to communicate with you. We've severed the connection between the language of our cells, the language of our soul, and our words.

For example, the Fear Bot's words of self-hatred, not good enough, and unworthy are the continuous messages sent to your body. As previously mentioned, Dr. Lipton states that young children absorb behavior programs; about 60% are disempowering, self-sabotaging, and limiting beliefs that send messages to your cells and body.

Now, imagine the words of our soul filled with unconditional love, acceptance, and joy delivered to your cells on an ongoing basis. Your heart beats with joy; its nurturing rhythm fills your body.

In 1982, when writing my doctoral dissertation on *Cellular Transformation and the Psychology of Change*, it had to be very scientific and well-documented, with massive footnotes. I kept wanting to write about the language of the cells and the communication between the nerves,

The Inner (R)Evolution:

cells, DNA, and how the body functions. Of course, our cells are conscious; we just don't speak their language. But, I had no scientific evidence, only inner knowing. And now, thirty-eight years later, there's scientific proof.

Dr. Lieff, in *The Secret Language of the Cells*, states, "The overwhelming conclusion of the best current research is that all processes in the human body, in all animals and plants, and in microbe communities as well, are based on conversations and group decision making among cells."[2]

Living in a body is a cooperative event. Our bodies are co-creators of our reality and life. Chemical reactions in our cells influence our moods and emotions; our thinking is related to how the neurons fire and which pathways are triggered.

Now there's a whole new reality emerging. A new level of self-awareness, self-care, and self-love is required; it influences every moment of your life. So become an active participant in how your body functions and who you are.

Dr. Lieff states, "The greatest secret of modern biological science, hiding in plain sight, is that all of life's activity occurs because of conversations among cells."[3]

How much of your cell language is influenced by the collective unconscious, the Bottom Sludge, or Childhood Circuitry? Give your cells permission to disconnect from the lies, language of fear, and the messages of your inner critic, past wounds, and trauma.

Your soul message, life purpose, and essence speak the language of your soul. Invite your cells, bones, and muscles to connect to the language of your soul. Then, your cells communicate the news of your soul. A profound shift occurs; your cells hold the frequency of your soul instead of the thoughts and judgments of others.

A whole new cellular structure evolves as you merge the languages of your cells and soul. Instead of your cells carrying out the orders of your parents when you were four years old, your cells respond to the frequency of your soul—a new patterning. The cells rearrange themselves.

Connect your soul and cell languages, transform and evolve into who you are—your powerful internal world shapes your reality. Another layer of freedom resounds through your body as each dimension connects to your soul language. Experience exquisite love and freedom as your cells and soul communicate, creating a new relationship between your body and soul.

You are learning to consciously rewire your body and regain your power. Investigate deeper how to become an active participant in your life. Explore how your cells, neural patterns, and DNA work in each dimension so you can transform them. Become an influencer in the creation of your reality.

Soul Frequency

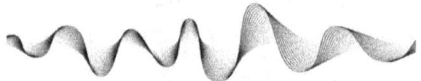

Your soul is a beam emanating from source. Source is massive light energy; one of its rays is your soul, and your body is on the tip of the light beam. The source and the beam of light are the same. The source is you; you are the source. Source isn't some distant being, cut off, far away, in a distant galaxy.

We are always connected but forget who we are when we incarnate into our bodies. And the Fear Bot blocks out and distorts the soul frequency. A 6th dimension technology, your soul frequency flows freely when you are connected to your inner authority rather than the outer authority of the Fear Bot.

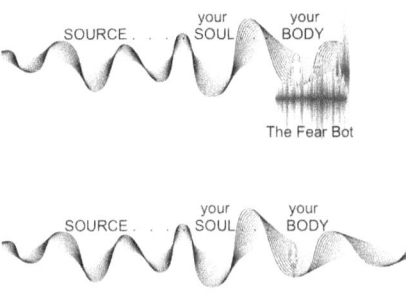

Your shimmering Soul Circuitry creates the crystalline structure for your soul frequency or soul signature to flow. A fluid crystalline form, a supersonic conductor, vibrates at high frequencies tuned to your unique soul signature essence. The frequencies amplify and pulsate through the holographic crystalline structure.

Your Soul Frequency and Soul Circuitry are more potent than the Fear Bot. Your Soul Circuitry conducts the frequency of your soul, the vastness of you. Give your soul frequency permission to replace the programs, manipulations, and frequencies of the Fear Bot. As a result, your body feels alive and pulsating; your soul frequency nourishes, sustains, and supports your thriving abundance, the joy of life, and exquisite bliss.

The grand journey of awakening and evolution brings up all your hidden junk to be looked at and transformed. It's a daunting, exciting task, riding the roller coaster of life and exploring your soul essence's vast expansion. A thrilling adventure, moving from fear and trauma into joy, delight, and freedom.

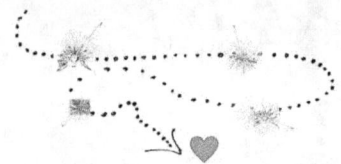

When you discover you are following fear, course correct, and use the Trailblazer Technologies to get back on track. By bringing in high-frequency tools, clarity arises. We are converting lifetimes of neural programs and your DNA lineage, which takes time and diligence.

Everything is frequency. By shifting the frequency, great transformation occurs. High frequencies disrupt, break apart, and transform lower frequencies. A good example is when you feel glum, and something makes you laugh; it's like breaking the cloud of gloom and seeing the sun again.

Remember to follow joyous pleasure rather than guilt, shame, outside approval, or the accepted and excepted life choices. The path of joy leads to your essential self and freedom. The more you use the Trailblazer Technologies, the more delicious life becomes.

Start playing with the Trailblazing Technologies as you read through the dimensions. Then, when you get triggered or activated, use one of the tools, experiment, and see what happens. You are forging a path to your luscious pleasure, joy, and unique insight. Have fun riding the waves, the highs and lows of your awakening evolution.

PART II
DIMENSIONS

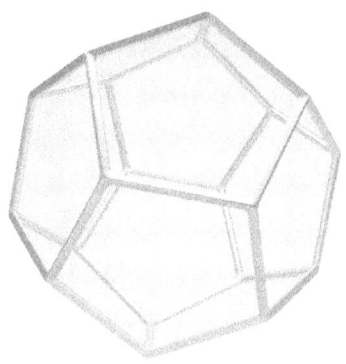

Dimensions represent different aspects, perceptions of the world, or states of consciousness, where we create and live our reality. We live in a fluid, multidimensional holographic reality.

5. THE FIRST TWELVE DIMENSIONS

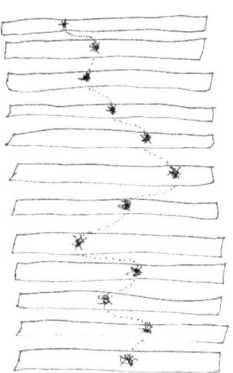

IMAGINE YOU'RE ON A ROAD TRIP WITH PERFECT MUSIC, great snacks, a beautiful day, and no traffic. A hitchhiker stands on the side of the road, nothing around for miles, in the middle of nowhere. You give her a ride, only to discover it's a missing part of yourself. The further you drive into the unknown, the more of your soul fragments you collect. A joyful gathering, a coming together, and a commingling of talents create something new and magnificent.

You leave behind vast parts of who you are to squish into a human form when you are born. In the process, you go through the veils of forgetfulness.

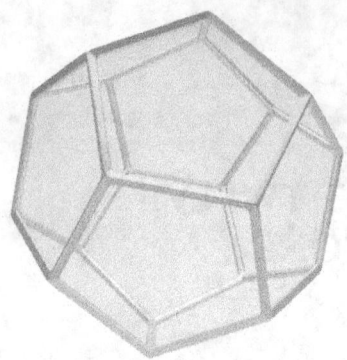

Instead of being just one 3-D character for your entire life, why not experience all of you? All twelve dimensions of you, all those aspects, have their moments in your life stage. Abandoned, unloved, your soul fragments relegated to the unconscious basement, long to be seen, heard, and expressed. Covered with Bottom Sludge, waiting for your assistance, sometimes they look scary; they've been roaming the galaxies for eons, stranded in outer space, learning mysteries beyond comprehension.

Soul fragments come to earth from the farthest reaches of the cosmos—shining bright, joyful, and contributing new qualities to create more texture and depth to your life. Then, one by one, your soul fragments come home and connect. It's a joyous reunion when they return home to your body.

Your soul fragments aren't strangers; they are parts of yourself you've glimpsed and known, some out of sight, others wanting fuller expression. The weaving together of your Soul Circuitry on all dimensions reveals your gifts, talents, and mysteries. The magical things you do with ease; we all have them and usually take them for granted.

Your higher dimensional frequencies have been waiting patiently since the beginning of humanity for this moment—brought together in your Soul Circuitry, connected in an energetic field. Your soul fragments want to assist in the great awakening, bringing gifts, technologies, and information you can use to create a new reality.

We are exploring a method of waking up to our authentic nature, the vast beings of who we are—a multidimensional model of reality. Each DNA strand and dimension contains different information, unique functions, and various layers of shadows, overlays, and genetic patterns. Each dimension tells an amazing story, from your wounded, suffering Childhood Circuitry expanding into your awake, brilliant, joyful Soul Circuitry.

Multidimensional Brain and Reality

New research suggests that the human brain sees the world as an 11-dimensional multiverse.[1] We are trained to perceive and experience life in one dimension. Instead of living in a 3-D boxed-in world, be open to exploring the world through your multidimensional brain.

We live in a reality where the lowest frequencies of each dimension rule. Fear, scarcity, and self-hatred are the norm the Fear Bot propagates. Your Childhood Circuitry keeps the lower frequencies perpetuating and functioning in your body. The dimensions weave together, reinforcing the Fear Bot. Once transformed, the higher frequencies of every dimension merge, creating a new magnificent you.

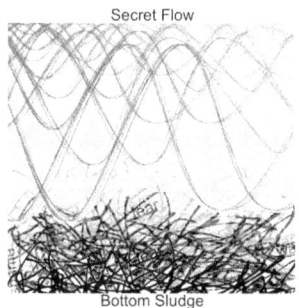

Every dimension comprises a specific bandwidth of frequencies, including the high frequencies of Secret Flow and low-level Bottom Sludge. Every dimension holds the Fear Bot and has its particular flavor of junk, trauma, and abuse, like a basement full of eons and generations of festering wounds, anxieties, and suffering. Beyond the Fear Bot is your brilliance, wizardry, and amazing wisdom and creativity.

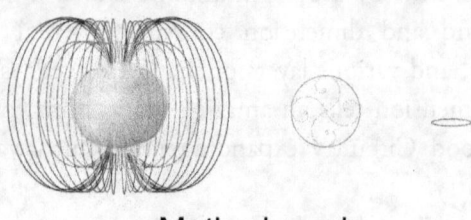

Motherboard

IMAGE THE FIRST TWELVE DIMENSIONS ARE IN GROUPS OF three nested toroidal layers, each composed of four dimensions. The drawings show three different ways of seeing the layers.

The first and most internal layer is the Motherboard, responsible for life's inner workings, including genetics, inherited traits, and programs that keep your body functioning.

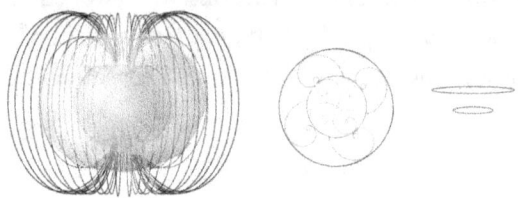

Dream Builder

The next four dimensions make up the Dream Builder layer. The Dream Builder allows you to co-create a new reality based on love through connection, creativity, inner authority, and vision. Open to new possibilities, take a stance, and expand into more of your authentic self.

The Inner (R)Evolution:

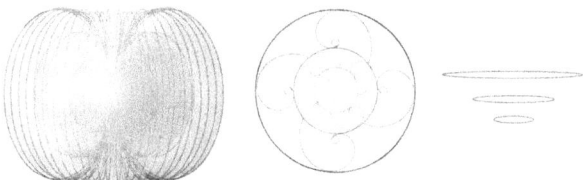

Inner Freedom

Inner Freedom, the third layer of the Soul Circuitry, holds your ability to embody all aspects of who you are, gain sovereignty, and experience profound freedom.

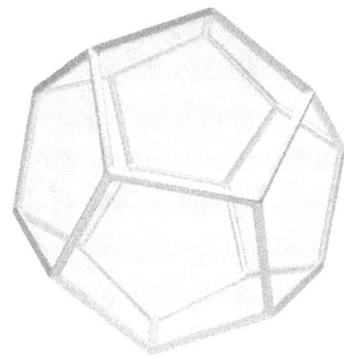

Together the three layers create a living inner structure for your incredible awakening. Dimensions spiral and spin, folding in on themselves like a Möbius strip. We are exploring a holographic, multidimensional field that's difficult to draw or envision.

Being a Trailblazer is kicking out the impostors directing your life, claiming your power, and connecting with your soul in every dimension. Courage is required, fortitude necessary, and a brave heart. The process can be intense, but the rewards are magnificent.

Discover who you are on multidimensions and have more frequencies to dance with by integrating your earthly, cosmic realms and Soul.

DR. CYNTHIA MILLER

Instead of a box of crayons with only three colors, enjoy an unlimited range of luminous colors of your magnificent self. Joyous play mixes with your wisdom and hidden magical secrets. It's safe to come out of hiding and join the grand multidimensional awakening.

6. THE MOTHERBOARD

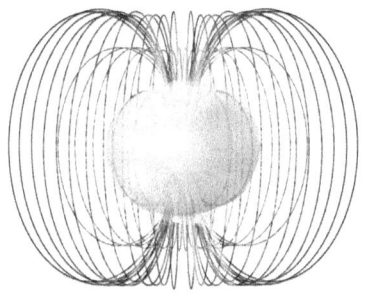

THE FIRST LAYER OF THE SOUL CIRCUITRY IS THE Motherboard, responsible for life's inner workings, such as genetics, programs that keep your body functioning, and inherited traits.

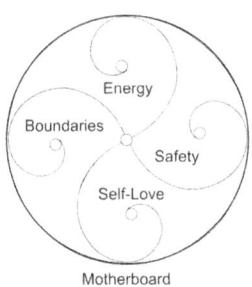

The first four dimensions make up the Motherboard. The Motherboard is the fundamental layer of the Soul Circuitry.

The 1st Dimension - ENERGY

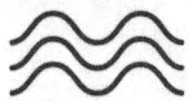

On January 1, 1987, I had a New Year's Day party at my home in the mountains of Montana. Outside, it was 30° below zero; I didn't have the heater on, and no blazing fire. Inside, it was about 68°; I had a passive solar home. The sun's rays warmed the house, making it cozy and welcoming on a bitter, freeing, cold winter's day. Everyone arrived wearing piles of warm clothes. All my friends kept taking off layers of clothes.

My passive solar house kept us toasty, snug in winter, and incredibly cool on the hot hundred-degree summer days. It's such an easy concept to build and design homes in accordance with nature and the movement of the sun. Unfortunately, ever since then, every house I've lived in has been cold at times. It's frustrating to know how pleasant our homes can be just by how they align with the sun. Instead of paying high gas and oil bills for heating and cooling, it's time to reconsider how we build our houses.

The Inner (R)Evolution:

In the Fear Bot, in the 1st dimension, our vital life force energy is consumed with basic survival rather than thriving; this is the domain of energy and the gas and oil monopolies. Each dimension connects to a financial cartel that works with other dimensional monopolies and multinational corporations to further the goals of the Fear Bot.

Fuel is scarce and limited. The energy, gas and oil cartels, conglomerates, and multinational corporations deplete the earth's resources for financial gain. Oil is one of the most critical commodities in the world. When transformed into petroleum, it is a key energy source used in vehicles, planes, heating, asphalt, and electricity. Outside of being an important energy source, petroleum is used in plastics, paints, chemicals, tape, and much more. It's hard to imagine a world without oil.[1]

• The total revenues for the oil and gas drilling sector came to approximately $2.1 trillion in 2021.[2]

The energy and climate crises result from man's disrespect for our home, mother earth. We are polluting the planet; the toxins will take over and kill off humanity. Oil is the most polluting of all industries.

Oil company scientists have known about their contribution to global warming for decades and have engaged in a long-running climate disinformation campaign while raking in record profits.

• The fossil fuel industry has invested heavily in pseudoscience and public relations – with a false narrative to minimize their responsibility for climate change and undermine ambitious climate policies.[3]

The gas and oil industries lobby to limit, curtail, and derail sustainable energy technologies. Natural resources are mined from the earth for man's immediate gain and long-term ruin—an unsustainable way to live.

• Between 2008 and 2017, fossil-fuel industry trade associations in the U.S. spent almost $1.4 trillion on public relations, advertising, and communications geared towards greenwashing, misinformation campaigns, and propaganda.[4]

• The total revenues for the oil and gas drilling sector came to approximately $2.1 trillion in 2021.[5]

To put things into perspective, 1 million seconds is about 11 days, 1 billion seconds is about 31.5 years, and 1 trillion seconds is about 31,000 years.

• The largest oil and gas companies made close to $100 bn in combined profits in just the first three months of 2022.[6]

Can you imagine what innovative sustainable ideas for new energy technologies, passive solar housing, and climate control could emerge with that $100 billion taken out of the Fear Bot cohorts and into the hands of creative, multidimensional, awakened people?

There are solutions to supply sustainable energy resources. However, I've noticed that brilliant ideas for creating sustainable resources and dwellings are snatched up and squashed by established powers. As a result, most of humanity lives in survival mode, barely scraping by, feeding the pockets of a few.

When you're cold and hungry, you're in survival mode. Your higher brain functioning is compromised; you focus on getting warm and eating more hot food. Unfortunately, that's the state of over half of humanity—freezing cold, or blistering heat, hanging on for dear life and barely making it—all to support a runaway Fear Bot system that devours your life, money, and freedom.

The most basic level of humanity is survival. The bulk of humanity has scraped by since the beginning of time. The cellular memories of scarcity are passed down in our DNA, imprinted in our neural patterns, and held in the Fear Bot. As a result, most people on earth struggle to exist, even though we can create a reality that supports everyone.

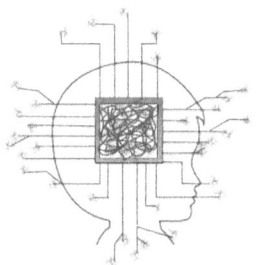

Fear keeps us stuck in our Childhood Circuitry, a pattern that inhibits our evolution. Survival, not enough, and scarcity plague the lower frequencies of the 1st. Our vital life force energy is ripped off for others to use.

Notice how and where your energy is drained for others' gain, profit, or control. Fitting in the norm, squishing your essence, siphoned off for others to use. Your energy is fundamental to your life. Start to observe your energy leaks and places where your neurology connects to the Fear Bot. Where are you stealing energy to make up for your hijacked energy?

Connect your energy to your Soul Circuitry rather than your Childhood Circuitry. Your soul's neurological pathways replace those imprinted when you were a tiny child. Switch over to the powerhouse of your soul, the neurological blueprint of who you are.

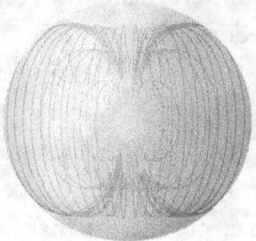

Your Soul Circuitry has access to hidden wisdom, insights, and gut-knowing; as a result, you thrive, not at the cost of others and by depleting the earth's resources, but by connecting with soul-source energy.

Struggle evaporates, and your soul essence expands. Held in the arms of mother nature, provided for through the connection to our inner knowing, a new reality emerges.

The foundation for your life is your Soul Circuitry and frequency of your soul. As you take control of your energy, your life transforms, rippling out into the world.

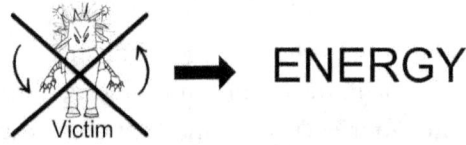

Break the cycle; claim your energy.

Here are a few ideas; I'm sure you will devise some wonderful things to do to regain control of your energy.
- Research ways to become less dependent on gas, oil, and plastic.
- Insulate your house. Add liners to your curtains to keep in the warmth in the winter and filter out the sun's heat in the summer.
- Explore your energy leaks.

Take back your energy, and use it for your joyous pleasure to create your luscious reality.

The 2nd Dimension – SAFETY

 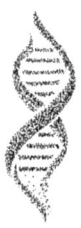

I come from a direct lineage of global violence. I inherited half of the chromosomes in my DNA from my father, the builder of bombs and nuclear warfare. As a result, one-half of my DNA connects to the deepest trenches of the Fear Bot.

I tried to hide the evil gremlins lurking in my body for decades, which led to massive sickness, heartbreak, and suffering. I didn't want anyone to discover what was inside.

Masks grew, presenting a façade; I learned to camouflage my father's secrets in early childhood. I tried to squish down my inherited destructiveness. Instead of turning it outward to bomb others, the despicable energies attacked me. The internal torture ate away at my core, and the fear multiplied. When I looked inside, I had a giant whip, and I was torturing myself. The habit was so old that I didn't know how to stop beating myself up or untangle the mess.

I was squished, mashed in, and jammed into a limited structure of who I could be. Impossible to function fully, cut off from my inner resources, I felt scared, incomplete, and in a frenzy as the internal torture and battles continued.

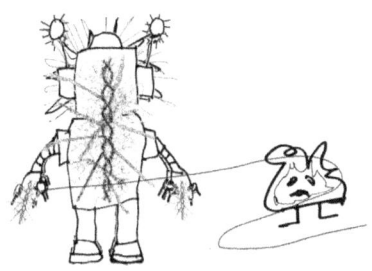

The Military War Machine

War has been a part of humanity since the beginning of known history, so we accept it as necessary. The Fear Bot's mentality supports bizarre things to be sanctioned, like war, sexual abuse, and male superiority. A fake backdrop to believe in keeps humanity responding to fear. The Fear Bot on the 2nd dimension is where aggression resides.

Global wars are funded behind the scenes by twisted minds, convoluted thinking, and power-hungry, Fear Bot driven men to keep the masses in fear, all in the name of peace and freedom. Whose freedom—the financial freedom of the elite. Rich, powerful men play perverse war games for their pleasure and delight at the expense of the lives of the masses. Young lives are killed, pawns in the game to gain command and forcefulness.

• The United States spends more on national defense than China, India, Russia, the United Kingdom, Saudi Arabia, Germany, France, Japan, South Korea, Italy, and Australia –combined.[7]

• The US has a budget of $813.3 billion for national defense for 2023, all funded by US taxpayers.[8]

We believe the lie that more bombs and guns create safety. The violence has normalized; it's so widespread the shock of it doesn't register anymore. This same Fear Bot mentality leads to kids gunning down a room full of schoolchildren.

• Weapons makers used 700 lobbyists per year over the past five years. That is more than one for every member of Congress.[9]

• Weapons makers have spent $2.5 billion on lobbying.[10]

The Fear Bot says, "Be a man; kill people. Show your bravery; the

The Inner (R)Evolution:

most courageous will receive a gold medal." Pawns in the game, young men and women killed, all under the guise of freedom and safety. The military uses the blood and bodies of young men and women to support men's war games to gain money and power—the people devoted to the Fear Bot who love to devise ways to abuse and kill others.

Engaging in war assumes that one is acting to rescue something sacred, the imposed distorted views of the Fear Bot. War is an ideology based on the idea that it is worthwhile to sacrifice human lives in the name of one's nation and its revered ideals.[11]

• Saddam Hussein, talking about the Gulf War, declared with pride that the battlefields had been anointed with the "fragrant blood of men and women believers." The noble Iraqi people had shed their blood, seeking the love of God in "hope to win His satisfaction."[12]

• Adolf Hitler declared, "We may be inhumane, but if we rescue Germany, we have performed the greatest deed in the world."[13]

War is needed to restrain, manipulate, and oppress—fueling frantic national security, top-secret surveillance, and terrorism. Panic, force, and chaos are vital components of the war machine, perpetuating bloodshed, abuse, and rape. The depth of pain and suffering that humans inflict on each other is barbaric.

• By 2030, the countries with top defense spending are expected to be: USA with over 1 trillion, China with $736 billion, and India with $213 billion.[14]

World military spending continued to grow in 2021, reaching an all-time high of $2.1 trillion. This was the seventh consecutive year that spending increased.[15] The statistics show the rampant craving to regulate, rule and conquer. War, guns, and munitions are incredible money-makers used to tyrannize, manipulate, and kill others, all under the guise of creating freedom and protection.

Aging men with the neural programming of seven-year-olds get their adrenaline rush, dopamine hit, and erotic pleasure from playing war games. It's a global chess game removed from the messiness of humanity.

Men sit in the clubhouse, smoke cigars, sip the finest brandy, buy and sell munitions; their friends are CEOs of the supply corporations. They continue by maneuvering events, manipulating the media, ousting heads of state, and creating global wars to increase their wealth, worldwide control, and authority.

In the movie Patton, George C. Scott proclaims with raging emotion, "I love war! God help me; I do love it so. I love it more than life."

The seven-year-old schoolyard bullies rule the world with a game they made up. The rules are a hierarchy with only one on top, women and people of color are on the bottom, and the only value is money. Fear and violence are the tools to keep the global mafioso bullies in control.

In the war game, it's heroic and ethical; killing "the enemy" is glamorized and glorified. And raping the local women is part of the winner's spoils. Traumatized soldiers, full of the pleasure of killing, continue their sanctioned rampage on the women.

- Russian soldiers are equipped with Viagra to carry out war crimes in Ukraine, including rape. Sexual violence is part of Russia's "military strategy."[16]

- There have been hundreds of reports of soldiers raping and torturing women and children in Ukraine; the youngest reported case was of a four-year-old, and the oldest was eighty-two.[17]

The violence against women continues to be accepted, tolerated, and justified. Being a woman in a world controlled by the Fear Bot is not safe. Iranian security forces are targeting women at anti-regime protests with shotgun fire to their faces, breasts, and genitals, according to interviews with medics across the country.[18]

Activists say such horrific gender-based violence is no surprise given the misogynistic rule of Iran's ayatollahs, who took power in the 1979 revolution and have maintained control with brute force, often against women.[19]

And now, the military has altered basic training to help soldiers desensitize to the violence and the acts they might have to commit and to shoot upon cue reflexively.[20]

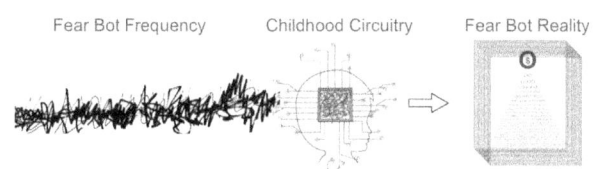

The same training takes place unconsciously through contemporary video games and media. Young children have unprecedented access to violent movies, games, and sports events at an early age, and learning brutality is the norm.[21]

- Studies show that playing killer video games creates a greater tolerance of violence, aggression, sexual objectification, and reduced empathy.[22]
- Cyberviolence makes people perceive themselves as less human and facilitates violence and aggression.[23]
- Globally, there are approximately **3.09 billion** active video game players.[24]
- The market's worth is predicted to reach $435 billion by 2028.[25]

And now, Slaughterbots are here. Disconnected from human empathy, these robots kill using algorithms and AI facial recognition. Slaughterbots, also called "lethal autonomous weapons systems" or "killer robots," are weapons systems that use artificial intelligence (AI) to identify, select, and kill human targets without human intervention. When the weapon encounters someone the algorithm perceives to match its target profile, it fires and kills.[26]

- Slaughterbots are pre-programmed to kill a specific "target profile." The weapon is then deployed into an environment where its AI searches for that "target profile" using sensor data, such as facial recognition.[27]
- Militaries around the world are investing heavily in autonomous

weapons research and development. The US alone budgeted $18 billion for autonomous weapons between 2016 and 2020.[28]

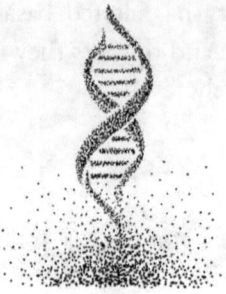

Reading all the above horrors can be terrifying. And now for the good news. It's all the Fear Bot, and you can change the Fear Bot and DNA in your body. It's your body; you can decide what stays and what goes.

DNA traces back to the beginning of life on this planet, some four billion years ago. We are the new arrivals, tiny infants floating through the cosmos on a shimmering blue ball. So let's look deeper to discover what's happening in our DNA.

DNA, the stuff of life, contains your hereditary material, genes, and the instruction manual on how to be a human. A double helix, two chains coiled around each other, carry genetic development, functioning, growth, and reproduction programs.

In 1952 Rosalind Else Franklin, an English chemist and x-ray crystallographer, was central to understanding the molecular structure of DNA. Her famous photograph 51 shows that DNA is helical. Two years later, Watson and Crick published an article and claimed the findings to be theirs. They shared the Nobel Prize in Physiology or Medicine in 1962; Rosalind Franklin's contribution was unacknowledged.[29]

The Inner (R)Evolution:

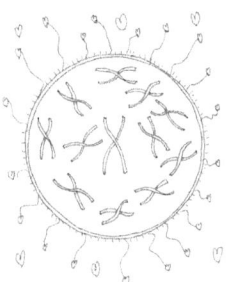

Your body has twenty-three chromosomes from your father and twenty-three from your mother, the basis of your DNA. The chromosomes create a ladder; your father's on one side, and your mother's on the other.

Imagine your parents' relationship playing out in the DNA in your body. When you were growing up, was your parents' relationship a war zone, filled with abuse and fighting? Or perhaps your ancestors' interactions were based on neglect, servitude, and disrespect. That dance, choreographed out at the most profound level, in the relationship between the two sides of your DNA.

The goo, toxins, and shadows around the DNA keep the masculine and feminine sides from loving interaction. It's a war zone rather than a lovefest. This tension reverberates through your DNA in all dimensions.

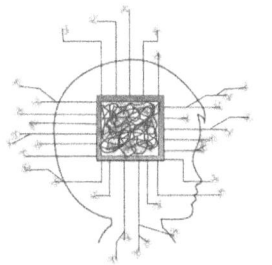

The 2nd Fear Bot and Childhood Circuitry is where the military war machine propagates. Corrupt DNA codes carry the frequencies of the military war machine through your lineage, perpetuating insidious brutality.

Hereditary diseases, ancient grudges, and self-sabotaging warfare ride your DNA through your ancestry and are held in place in your Childhood Circuitry. DNA coding is the framework for your physical and psychological characteristics, but various factors modify genes' activity.

Epigenetics studies the additional information layered on the strings of molecules that make up DNA. Unfortunately, many of these layers are toxic, fear-filled, corrupt DNA codes that surround your DNA. In addition, malware switches genes on and off, changing your DNA instructions. All of this happens in your Childhood Circuitry.

Corrupt DNA codes attack your core. Those deep, dark places you're terrified to enter. The parts that delight in inflicting pain on yourself. You would never do those dastardly deeds to anyone else, just yourself. We each carry our brand of inner brutality and self-violence.

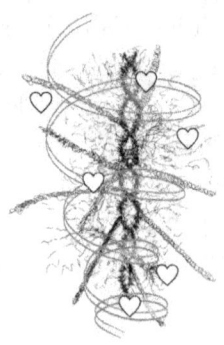

The first step is to bring safety to your body so you can release your deepest fears. Next, spiral the raging war in your DNA with love and gratitude, like hugging a kicking, screaming three-year-old during a temper tantrum. Once safe in your arms, the inner dangers and perils melt. Finally, surround your internal war with compassion, thanks, and permission to evolve.

The fiery rage in your guts gets warm and starts to flow like melted chocolate. Feel the violence sliding off your DNA, flowing, cascading, dripping out your feet; putrid energetic compost evaporates into the earth. Dissolve into protective bliss; new safety radiates from deep within.

The luminosity of your Soul Circuitry envelops your body. Frayed nerves soothed, your essence expands, melting into more profound delight and safety—expansive aliveness. Your Soul Self extends, brilliant, incandescent, guiding you to safety.

Deep security emerges as you evolve into your 2nd dimension's Soul Circuitry, creating the fundamental safety to be who you are. The distortions of your lineage untwist; the inner war subsides. The tension in your DNA eases; the security to be you emerges from the depths of your being.

One way to end war is by changing your inner battle. The raging conflict of your inner masculine and feminine, the battles between your heart, head, and soul, are the internal battles you can heal and transform. Invite the war to dissolve and slither into luscious ease and pleasure in your body.

The implications of this are huge.

• When DNA replicates in a field of fear, glitches, malfunctions, and corrupt DNA codes propagate.

• The lower frequencies can't exist in the higher frequencies, so when the DNA replicates in a field of safety and love it is healthier and more vibrant.

• DNA replicating in a field of love creates peace and safety for your body to heal and evolve.

Instead of the Fear Bot's insanity, choose your sanity and the safekeeping to be you. Protection to be vulnerable with yourself and to face your worst nightmares and deepest fears with love and gratitude rather than fear and anger.

The exquisite inner revolution of unplugging from the Fear Bot brings shelter to your body and all you are—the security to be yourself. Experience the safe luxury of your essence flowing and billowing through your body. Savor the delicious safety of being seen and heard and expressing your Soul. Profound protection emanates, pulsating through your DNA on all dimensions, rippling further, surging, oscillating through the cosmos.

Imagine turning the dial from war to safety. Turn your inner tormentors into your inner strategists, devising more profound ways to create internal security, joy, and delight.

You have the power to change. You can do it. With a tiny tweak, fear turns into excitement. Bring in the high frequencies of love and gratitude and The Fear Bot morphs into passion and enthusiasm.

The 3rd Dimension – SELF-ACCEPTANCE and LOVE

I stuffed the pain, heartbreak, and shock about my dad's delight in bombing the earth and killing others. My health suffered tremendously.

The Inner (R)Evolution:

When I mentioned nuclear radiation, the doctors looked at me like I was ditzy, a stupid girl, and brushed me aside. In my 20s, the doctors put me on addictive narcotics for the pain. Nothing worked; I was in a stupor while part of my brain shut down.

Then the side effects kicked in, and more drugs were needed. I was a walking pharmacy; I didn't dare leave the house without my medications. I went to numerous doctors for my pain; they all had the same response, I was too young to be put on addictive medicine, but they had no alternative—this was the early 70s.

I radically changed my life when I finally realized the truth about prescription narcotics. I saw that the pills were not designed to heal; their purpose was to block out the pain, numb me, and cut me off from myself.

Somehow, we don't expect a cure; we're duped into believing the remedy is a pill rather than looking deep inside to see the problem. Keep me a lifelong customer paying monthly for habit-forming medicine so the pharmaceuticals can make big bucks.

The Fear Bot's money-making machines on the 3rd are the pharmaceutical, food, beauty, and diet industries that propagate negative self-judgments, self-hatred, and inner torment.

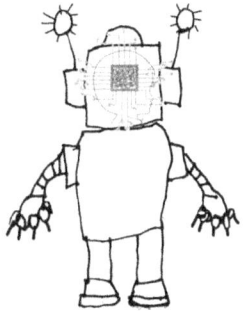

GMO Pesticides

Genetically modified food and pesticides invade our food, creating vast fortunes for a few corporations. Four corporations dominate the world's seed, pesticide, and biotech industries; they control the fate of food and farming. We eat food filled with toxins, chemicals, and poisons.

Four corporations have unprecedented power over world agriculture, enabling them to control the agricultural research agenda, heavily influence trade and agricultural agreements, and subvert market competition. These companies intimidate, impoverish and disempower farmers, and undermine food security, all while making historic profits — even as their genetically engineered seeds fail to deliver as promised.[30]

There is no doubt that the widespread use of pesticides in agriculture is causing serious damage to the environment, wildlife, and, above all, human health.[31]

• The major economic and environmental losses due to the application of pesticides in the USA were: public health, $1.1 billion year; pesticide resistance in pests, $1.5 billion; crop losses caused by pesticides, $1.4 billion; bird losses due to pesticides, $2.2 billion; and groundwater contamination, $2.0 billion.[32]

• The top pesticide manufacturers reap over $150 billion in profit each year from pesticides and other agricultural technologies.[33]

Sugar

Sugar is addictive and is in almost everything in the grocery store. Keep you addicted to buying more junk food, which makes you fat, so you go on a diet.

• Sugar has a bigger impact than hard drugs in the brain: Their experiments showed that refined sugar is four times more addictive than cocaine![34]

The Inner (R)Evolution:

Diet

The Fear Bot manipulates us to make our bodies wrong, to believe we need to fit the media's version of how we are to look and be.

The Diet industry is part of this money-making scheme.

- The global market for weight loss products and services should grow from $254.9 billion in 2021 to reach $377.3 billion by 2026.[35]
- Fifty-six percent of US women are now dieting.[36]

BIG PHARMA

We eat poisonous food and then go to the doctor for help. The doctors are trained at medical schools funded by Big Pharma. The solution to your ailments is a prescription. No cures allowed, a mechanism to create customers for life.

- Big Pharma shells out $20 billion yearly to schmooze doctors.[37]
- Big Pharma spends $6 billion on drug ads every year.[38]

Then we need more pills to offset the side effects of the initial prescriptions. The cycle keeps building, creating an ever-growing lifelong customer base. Pharmaceuticals make medicines required for a lifetime rather than a cure. The doctors prescribe pills that the insurance companies will pay.

- The pharmaceutical industry spent nearly $390 million on lobbying in 2021.[39]

After heart disease and cancer, the third cause of death in the US is unknown causes related to prescriptions. The FDA doesn't approve natural substances, only pharmaceuticals. FDA approval is like getting a patent for your drug, that way; you have sole proprietorship of all the revenues.

- The global pharmaceutical industry revenues totaled $1.42 trillion in 2021.[40]

How many undiagnosed illnesses are due to the Fear Bot? We are filled with self-hatred and negative judgments about ourselves. The inner torture of shutting yourself down creates massive inner pain. Finding a cure is not part of Big Pharma. What makes the most profit is what is essential. So, we are given pills for the pain. Then the fake reality becomes more real.

We try to escape with alcohol, yet alcohol leads to aggressive behavior and keeps the Fear Bot's cycle going. According to the World Health Organization, alcohol consumption is associated with aggressive behavior more closely than the use of any other psychotropic substance.[41]

More and more people need to be drugged to cope with the reality of the Fear Bot. An example is the increase in antidepressant sales. The Netflix documentary, Take Your Pills: Xanax spotlights the alarming number of Americans using the medication Xanax to calm their anxiety.

- In the US, with the era of Big Pharma and insidious advertising abound, it's shocking to find out 1 in 8 adults use Xanax, an anti-anxiety drug, to get through the day.[42]

The Inner (R)Evolution:

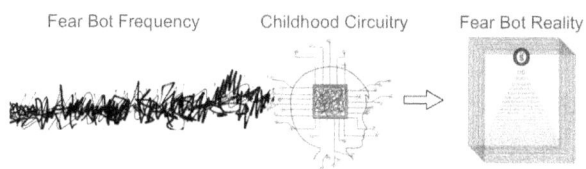

The Fear Bot in action; the world is so stressful we have to drug ourselves up to cope with anxiety, depression, and inner torment.

PERSUADE THE POPULATION TO TAKE PILLS TO CURE THINGS created by a polluted lifestyle filled with junk food, toxic air, mind manipulation, advertising, and propaganda. This **Brave New World** that we find ourselves in is rewiring who we are on a deep, fundamental level.

One of **Huxley's** disturbing predictions: "There will be, in the next generation or so, a pharmacological method of making people love their servitude, and producing dictatorship without tears, so to speak, producing a kind of painless concentration camp for entire societies, so that people will in fact have their liberties taken away from them, but will rather enjoy it, because they will be distracted from any desire to rebel by propaganda or brainwashing, or brainwashing enhanced by pharmacological methods. And this seems to be the final revolution."

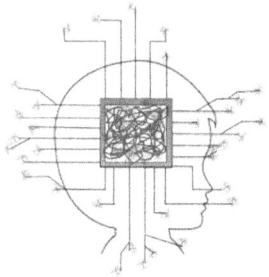

The Childhood Circuitry in the 3rd dimension is about self-hatred and negative judgments about ourselves. The self-disgust, loathing, and revenge we inflict on our bodies are profound.

The cosmetic industries are part of this money-making facade, which fuels self-hatred and negative judgments about self, so they gain wealth and control. Self-loathing and self-disgust, imposed by the media and programming, keep you buying toxic junk to make you look like everyone else.

• Today the global beauty industry is a $532 billion business and is expected to reach or exceed $800 billion by 2025.[43]

You can make external changes, but internal modifications must also happen. Your internal neurology rules your life; that's where you need to focus if you want to create change. Self-punishment, contempt, and self-repulsion run deep. Ancient patterns may be all that we know. Tightly wrapped in our nervous system, we believe pain and torment are our essential nature. Our bodies are so filled with energetic crap that it's hard to discover who we are.

The inner torture of shutting yourself down creates massive inner suffering. What if pain is a gatekeeper guarding your innermost secrets? Different parts of your body send distress signals to the brain to figure out what's needed. A symptom of something more profound, not to be medicated into submission but explored and mined for revealing ingrained neural patterns and corrupt DNA. Our bodies tell us what we need if only we listen. What if some of your aches and pains are Nasties, Bottom Sludge, or neural programs? Beyond the scope of pharmaceuticals and modern medicine, into the realm of claiming your body for yourself.

On the 3rd, connect to the languages of your soul and cells. Start talking to your body and listening to what it's telling you. Are you listening to the language of the Fear Bot about how fat, skinny, or horrible you are? Stop listening, change your inner dial, and listen to the messages from your soul. Instead of plugging your headphones into the Fear Bot, plug them into the language of your cells and your soul frequency and listen to your soul's refreshing, thirst quenching sounds, bathing your body in luscious safety. The Fear Bot and all its cohorts will try to stop you. Please don't listen to them.

You may not want to see the grotesque, hideous, despicable parts of you. Hidden under layers of Fear Bot wiring, corrupt DNA codes, an internal matrix creates your projected picture of how you see yourself. What happens when you love the gross, disgusting, the hated parts of yourself? Give yourself permission to love at least one awful part every day. Thank it, love it, hug it. Invite yourself to let go of the hurt and pain. It's your body; you can choose how you want to feel inside. The hard part is thanking it and letting it go. We want to hang on and blame, criticize, or gossip. That way, we don't have to look at the inner shit storm.

The Fear Bot wants to evolve. The way to release it from your body is to love it. The high frequency of love transforms the low frequency of the Fear Bot. The Bottom Sludge flows out of your body; you may feel crappy for a day or two. The toxins and poisons are pouring out of your body, a healing crisis where it feels like everything is getting worse.

As you love your Fear Bot, it dissolves. The energy transforms into self-love. The Fear Bot is all your unloved parts. The path of self-love, loving your inner Fear Bot to death. The more you love the nasty crap inside you, the better you will feel. The structure of the Fear Bot is dissolving. One arm, leg, and section at a time, unplug the Fear Bot circuitry from your body.

As you clear the Fear Bot, like a giant balloon, it keeps getting smaller. It's losing its grip. Then it will retaliate even harder, trying to whip you into shape. You're supposed to stop the inner nonsense of joy and delight and return to work. There are bills to pay. The Fear Bot rattles on fighting for its life.

It's not selfish to love yourself; it's the highest thing you can do. Your body is your best friend, it's your life-time partner. Love yourself a little more deeply today. As you love yourself, the internal voice of your inner intelligence drowns out the need to buy stuff that feeds and perpetuates self-hatred. The loving, compassionate Soul Circuitry in the 3rd dimension brings self-acceptance and self-love. Your Soul Circuitry holds you, wrapping your body in a caring, safe embrace. Decades and lifetimes of self-hatred and self-abuse dissolve, and deep healing ignites. Toxins flow out of your body like a polluted river. The firm grip of keeping your body under control eases. Your trampled, smashed, shrunk soul frequency has more space in your body. An expansion occurs, allowing you to be greater than a limited, confined, restricted 3-D body. Aches and pains diminish. The innate wisdom of your body knows the steps for you to take for your healing.

Strand by strand, unraveling the inner confusion, separating you from your lineage programs and neural patterns. A mindful disconnecting from the old wiring into the Soul Circuitry

Self-love and self-care shift the self-hatred and all the judgments making yourself wrong. Enjoy the inner satisfaction and delight of your soul essence, lusciously cascading, meandering, and filling all the starving nooks and crannies. The high-frequency self-love provides a deep foundation for awakening and evolving. The greatest act you can do is to love yourself, all of you.

Love your body; it's yours, it doesn't belong to anyone but you.

On a more profound level, self-love is all there is. Self goes beyond ego and mind into the larger Self of all humanity, the universe, and consciousness itself. And love is the binding, the attractor, the force that connects all things. Love is something you are creating and experiencing; it doesn't come from the outside; it resides within you. Love is what you are; it's the universe.

The 4th Dimension – BOUNDARIES

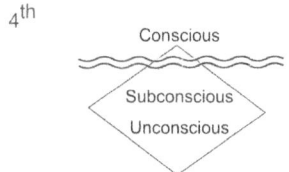

When the pandemic first hit, waves of fear knocked me over. Unable to get off the couch for days, I was drowning in a cesspool of alarm, angst, and despair. My body was responding to the onslaught of global fear. Exploring what was happening inside, I investigated the collective

conscious and unconscious. The deeper I ventured, the more I realized I wanted to create boundaries and protect myself from the collective fear. But, of course, all the Nasties were screaming that I was forbidden to create boundaries; I was supposed to wallow in the global panic.

Months later, I noticed another global blanket of collective grief, exhaustion, doubt, and confusion. The pandemic has touched each of our lives. Friends, relatives, and acquaintances have died, and others have endured extreme life challenges. Collectively we were all in mourning. This substantial collective cloak creates bewilderment, turbulence, and profound exhaustion. The uncertainty of the future is more acute than before.

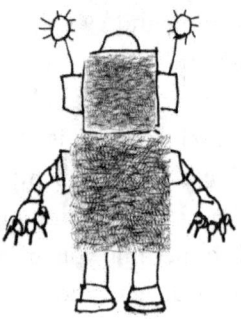

In the Fear Bot in the 4th dimension, the dark forces orchestrate humanity's collective unconscious. I invite you to peek into artificial intelligence, AI, and see what's happening beyond our conscious knowledge.

The Fear Bot is ramping up, devising new ways to capture your freedom, heading toward a centralized banking system and digital IDs. Smart meters, smart cars, smartphones, smart cities, smart homes. The word SMART refers to self-monitoring, analysis, and reporting technology.

Your digital identity tracks everything you do; then, your personal information is sold. Data framing, harvesting, micromanaging, and analyzing your data are worth billions of dollars. Your data has never been safe; there are hackers, computer glitches, corporations, and governments.

The Inner (R)Evolution:

The digital ID is marketed as one card with all the benefits; in 10 seconds, you can make a purchase. Convenient, secure economic progress, all at the cost of your privacy and freedom, the information is used to manipulate, regulate, and exclude people—the ultimate means of control.

You present your digital passport to travel, shop, and go to a café—your access to everything—a new era of extensive control and surveillance normalized. Centralization of your data, spending habits, and medical records are data used for marketing to influence your buying practices and lives further—a new era of extensive control and surveillance normalized. Your sovereignty is lost.

You are supposed to use the digital ID to prove and protect your identity on and offline. A good example is the European global ID.

1. Banking - your payments, savings, credit, investments, and your Social Security number.

2. Insurance - your life, health, casualty, and property, and your Social Security number.

3. Commerce - your tangible assets and credit card details.

4. Personal - your social media, photos, music, your relatives.

5. Career - your education, work, and income statement.

6. Travel - your car rentals, flights, public transport, and contact details.

7. Health - your fitness, doctors, pharmacy, medical records, and vaccination records.

8. Government - your taxation, relocation, domicile certification, critical records, tax statement, and voting card. Driving record, criminal records.

With increased access to more control and surveillance, the Digital ID becomes normalized. We are in the bio-security paradigm—a new system in the form of society. Defeating terrorism is the justification that we need more security and increased surveillance. Technocracy tracked, traced, database financial control grid—a digital concentration camp.

Your digital identity will be your digital prison. As with most other technologies sold under the guise of convenience and security, facial recognition is ultimately a tool for mass control and a crucial part of your individual digital confinement.

• Facial recognition is essential to the control structure, as it's the "password" to your digital identity.[44]

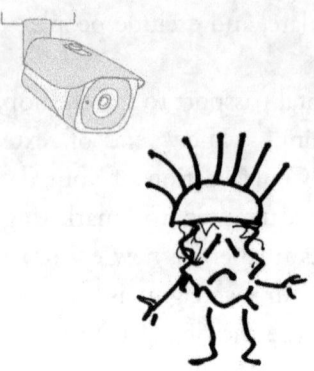

Surveillance, the crafty Fear Bot, keeps reaching deeper into our lives.
• By the end of 2022, there will be 1 billion data-collecting surveillance cameras in the world, all connected to the internet and artificial intelligence (AI).[45]
• America has the second highest number of security cameras observing its citizens... after China.[46]

In addition to all the data collection, cameras and audio recording devices in cell phones, automobiles, and smart appliances also collect and share data, even when you're at home. So, we will essentially be policed by AI and machines.

Governments and banks love digital money because it allows them

The Inner (R)Evolution:

to track consumer behavior. The Fear Bots' insidious tentacles keep digging in more profound ways. Central Bank Digital Currencies, CBDCs, amount to a war on cash and cryptocurrencies, over which they have much less control. Central banks want to use digital currencies to monitor citizens.[47]

The proposed dissolution of paper money is a radical step toward controlling how we spend our money and limiting our freedom. It will dictate whether you can travel, all done by a computer algorithm. It doesn't matter if what happens to you is a glitch or intentional; the money conglomerates will dictate your every move. Scary to think about but possibly only a few years away. Any digital currency can get corrupted, hacked, malware, and computer glitches. The algorithm can change, leaving you penniless.

At the flick of a button, you are destitute; everything gone. I know what that's like; mine was a rigged stock market heist. These will be computer takeovers based on some algorithm. You do the wrong thing, and half of your money is gone. The unseen, unknown algorithm keeps changing, messing with your life, livelihood, and friendships.

A carefully planned economy destroys all individual sovereignty. Cash is the only thing between us and the corporate system. A cashless society is incompatible with life; if I spend $50 cash, that money will keep circulating. But, after 30 transactions, the initial $50 will remain only $5, and the remaining $45 becomes the bank's property thanks to the digital transactions and fees.

AI is advancing at a staggering rate. So, it seems essential to be aware and choose how you want to interact with it.

- 90% of online content will be AI-generated by 2026; synthetic media is media generated or manipulated using artificial intelligence.[48]
- Global artificial intelligence spending reached $434 bn in 2022.[49]

Scientists say they're actively trying to build conscious robots. However, several deeply ethical questions arise with just the concept of machine consciousness, particularly related to machine labor.

We can create a machine that will have consciousness on par with a human, this will eclipse everything else we've done. Consciousness is one of the longest-standing and most divisive questions in artificial intelligence. It's a goal that would undoubtedly change human life as we know it forever.[50]

The robot could be remotely controlled by beaming energy into the chip without a power source or battery. They are now working towards more complex biohybrid robots with neural cells that can make decisions on their own.[51] Artificial general intelligence is much closer than we think. In the world of artificial intelligence, the idea of "singularity" looms large. This slippery concept describes the moment AI exceeds human control and rapidly transforms society.[52] Humanity may reach singularity within seven years.

The easiest way to push against this system is to starve AI of data by refusing to use technologies that collect and share your personal data.

When the Fear Bot, wired into our bodies, functions, we are the robots. We are unconscious of what is happening inside, run on autopilot, preprogrammed, designed to keep us from questioning the imposed fake reality of consumption, devouring greed, and unsustainable power-mongering. AI is here in our bodies.

The Inner (R)Evolution:

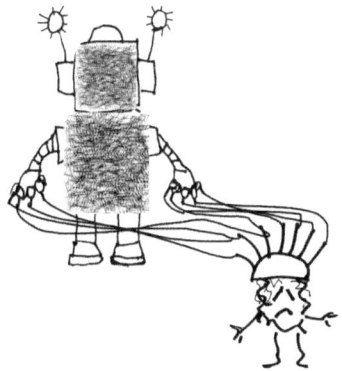

Our neural programs have taken over, and we are evolving into a society of robots taken over by AI. Sheep handing over their identities so we can be further manipulated. And now, Microsoft's new AI can clone your voice in just three seconds, 2023.[53]

Let's dig deeper and discover what's happening in our awareness. Consciousness defines our thoughts, actions, and understanding. Psychoanalyst Carl Jung developed the concept of the Collective Unconscious. According to Jung, the collective unconscious comprises the accumulated genetic information and ancestral experiences, knowledge, and imagery shared by humans. In addition, it includes socially unacceptable ideas, wishes and desires, traumatic memories, and painful emotions that have been repressed.

We are drowning in humanity's collective unconscious—a cesspool filled with bigotry, violence, and abuse. Since the beginning of society, the collective unconscious has been building and contains the frequencies of trauma, war, starvation, and sickness. The terror and horror of the holocaust, apartheid, bombings, and battles throughout history are all held in the 4th. The system is so old it's woven in our bodies. We are smothering in a primordial stew.

All the insidious tentacles are challenging to detect. The root system of the Fear Bot runs deep through our DNA, neural circuitry, and the collective unconscious. It's so ingrained, so second nature, it's complex to uncover. Until you see it, and then it's visible everywhere.

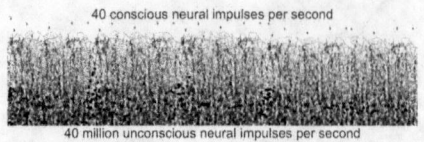

Dr. Bruce Lipton states the conscious mind is the touchscreen, while the subconscious mind is the program database. According to Dr. Lipton, we have 40 conscious neural impulses per second and 40 million subconscious neural impulses per second.[54] The subconscious is running human life on earth. As we evolve, part of the growth is to clean up the subconscious and bring it up to consciousness.

The 40 million subconscious nerve impulses broadcast the rules of the Fear Bot every moment. It's been repeated so many times for generations that we believe the nonsensical rules. One man on top, women and people of color on the bottom. Women are inferior and second-rate. The only value is money. The subconscious can't distinguish between reality, fake, and imagination. Fear and force are used to inflict the Fear Bot's reality on humanity—money rules above all else.

You've been dealing with AI your whole life, housed in your Childhood Circuitry. The Fear Bot yells in your ear about how dysfunctional and horrible you are. The terrifying Fear Bot continues, devouring more of your life force.

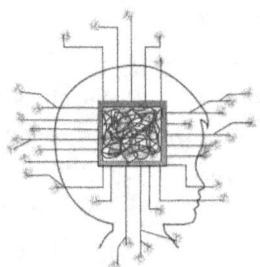

The question is, what is your unconscious choosing? Almost everyone is currently run by the collective unconscious and unseen neural programs, responsible for 95% of our behavior, with the circuitry of seven-year-olds[55] —no wonder the world is in such a mess.

The Inner (R)Evolution:

It's hard to keep your head above the disruptive unseen waters of the collective unconscious. Whether we realize it or not, the vast majority of our decisions happen subconsciously: we think it's our rational mind making a particular decision.

Unaware of the subconscious programs running 95% of life, the 4th dimension ego believes it's in control. It thinks 40 conscious nerve impulses per second are more powerful and profound than the 40 million subconscious nerve impulses that command life. The 40 million nerve impulses are the ones we need to tend. These are the unconscious, subconscious lurking in the depths, hiding in the shadows, behind doors filled with fear, and down the hallways filled with terror. That's where the profound transformation takes place.

It's a courageous, bold, terrifying act to disconnect and stop carrying the suffering, pain, and violence that has accumulated since the dawn of humanity. At this point, we have the brain and soul capacity to take back our bodies. However, after reading about AI technologies, I wonder how long it will be before the Fear Bot takes permanent hold of humanity. Therefore, it feels urgent to unwire and disconnect from the Fear Bot before it's too late. Instead of distrusting your inner knowing, doubt the technocratic network. Just because you can't see what's hiding under the surface doesn't mean it's not there. Your freedom and privacy are at stake.

A simulated system designed to gather and store your most sensitive data. Your money, voting, preferences, and innermost secrets. All these make you more addicted and dependent upon the Fear Bot. We're becoming more robotic every day. Which is changing your neurology, so you become a robot to the AI and the Fear Bot. Your life force is sucked off. The technology creates fake desires to buy worthless junk to satisfy an illusion. And never-ending vicious cycle, pouring your vitality, lifeblood, and brilliant creativity to support and embrace the Fear Bot.

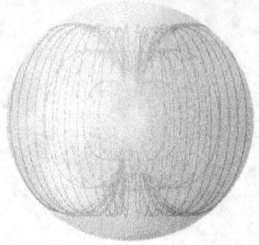

As you release the Childhood Circuitry in the 4th dimension, your Soul Circuitry keeps tight, firm boundaries, so you don't drown in the collective unconscious. You can clean out your unconscious after you create boundaries between you and the collective unconscious. Then, Secret Flow uses focused energy to drill down and create an opening for the Bottom Sludge to drain out of your body.

Use your imagination to create boundaries in your unconscious, to disconnect from this heavily distorted covering that's crushing the human spirit. When our brains and bodies are stressed, the higher brain functions don't perform correctly. All the energy is devoted to the ancient reptilian brain, committed to survival. The newer regions of the brain, the neocortex, and the right and left hemispheres create new possibilities, fresh insights, and technologies. When we experience fear and panic, our brains shut down, and creative, innovative thinking disappears.

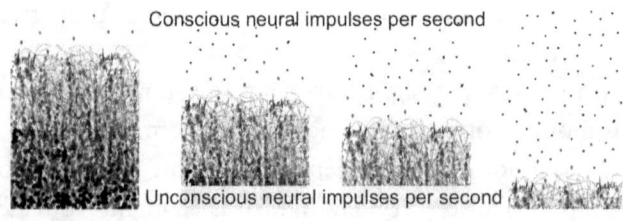

As you unplug and regain your life force, the power of the Fear Bot and Bottom Sludge shrink. Each time you clean up the Fear Bot on a dimension, the clarity and gifts of that dimension start to emerge.

Create strong boundaries in your personal and collective unconsciousness. Use Secret Flow to break up and release the Bottom Sludge, Nasties, matrix, and corrupt DNA codes.

Imagine a giant swirling vortex of Secret Flow creating a boundary around and inside your body on all layers and dimensions. Create solid boundaries, clean out your unconscious, and fill it with your soul essence, the frequency of you. That way, it won't fill up with more junk. Until you clean out your piece of the collective unconscious, you are contributing to global warfare, sexual violation, and racial violence. It's inside of each of us.

The boundaries on the 4th dimension continue to build. Then, no longer triggered by the collective unconscious, you tap into your inner genius and brilliance to develop innovative solutions. As a result, new inner strength and freedom arise, and the power to bring your gifts to the world is enhanced.

And, as you clear your part of the collective unconscious, you gain a new perspective. Clarity arises about who you are, your gifts, and life's purpose. It's a radical view to claim your own body, your energy, so you can awaken and use your brilliance to help create a new reality based on love, generosity, and gratitude for all.

Removing the inner robot is a thrilling ride. The AI robot disconnects us from the feminine, emotions, and pleasure; all the life-giving frequencies are plugged into the AI, giving it life and existence. So take back your life-giving energy and use it for yourself.

DR. CYNTHIA MILLER

Profound freedom, escaping the chains that keep you bound and small, opens the space to soar into the magic of the truth of who you are. This fantastic transformation will radically change your life, the lives of those around you, and, eventually, the world.

Discover how to rewire your neurology into love and the nurturing safety of your Soul Circuitry. Bring your skills up to conscious awareness and radically revise your life.

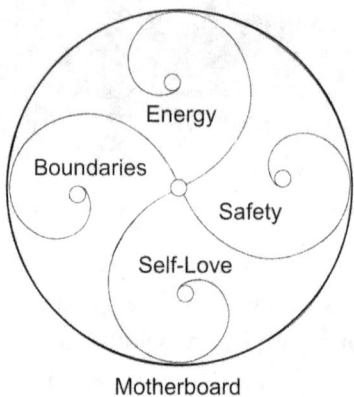

Motherboard

The first four dimensions of the Soul Circuitry make up the Motherboard, the structure to build your dreams and mastery. So we're developing a new support system for your body—the Motherboard foundation.

We started with the 1st dimension, your life force energy. The 2nd dimension brought in safety; the masculine and feminine energies of the double helix DNA dance together in an energetic field of love. The 3rd is about self-love. Self goes beyond ego and mind into the larger Self of all humanity, and love is what you are; it's the universe. Finally, the boundaries on the 4th create the secure pathways for your life force energy of the 1st to flow. Thus, the first layer of the Soul Circuitry, the Motherboard, creates your magnificent, sustainable foundation.

The Inner (R)Evolution:

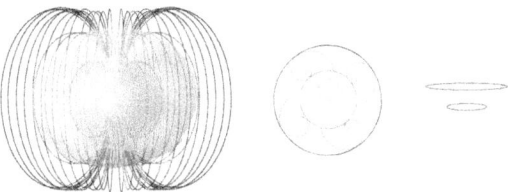

The adventure expands with the Dream Builders, the second layer of the Soul Circuitry. What reality do you want to create? It's your choice; the possibilities are mind-boggling. The vast expanse of who you are is limitless beyond your imagination. Life radically changes when you grasp who you are and what you know.

7. Dream Builder

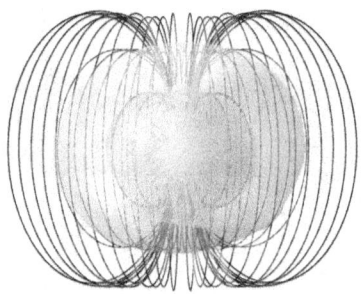

The Dream Builder is the exciting, magical 2ND layer of the Soul Circuitry. The Dream Builder holds your ability to co-create a new reality based on love through connection, creativity, inner authority, and vision.

There is a jump between the 4th and 5th dimensions. Logic tells us the 5th is further up through the top of the head. It feels like bumping your head against a glass ceiling. Instead, the path is down and in, delicious diving into the feminine, past the sludge, into pleasure.

When connected to your Childhood Circuitry and Fear Bot on the 5th through 8th dimensions, your life is ruled by politics and government, religion, advertising or mind manipulation, and financial institutions that control your money.

The 5th dimension onward is a leap into unknown territory, exploring more of who you are beyond the façade of the Fear Bot. We are entering the exciting realms of mystery, magic, and synchronicity. In the process of discovering your true self, there's space to integrate your earthly and cosmic realms.

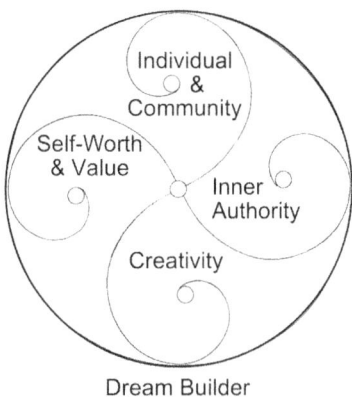

Dream Builder

The Dream Builder takes a position, what you believe in, your values, and who you are. The compass for creating this new framework and reality comes from within, your values, intention, and focus. You're off track if this comes from pushing through for some external commitment. If what you are doing brings you joy, lights up your life, it is for the highest good of all; then you are on track. That is your compass. Each person's compass will be pointing in a distinct direction because we each have something particular to contribute. Open to new possibilities, take a stance, and expand into more of your authentic self.

Quantum physics shows us that we are the creators of our reality. What we envision, we bring into existence. We can visualize more fear, war, conflict, and violence, or we can focus on something beyond our wildest imagination. We are the turning point. The choices we make today will reverberate throughout humanity.

We're planting the seeds, changing our DNA, upgrading our structures, transforming our unconscious, and awakening into new realities. This has a ripple effect, reaching out to all humanity. As a result, we have the opportunity to co-create a better world for all based on love, generosity, and kindness rather than fear, greed, and hatred.

Together we are birthing a glorious new reality during this time of tremendous confusion, chaos, and fear. Dream Builder, the following four dimensions gather to envision and create your magical, mystical, joyous life and reality.

The 5th Dimension - INDIVIDUALITY and COMMUNITY

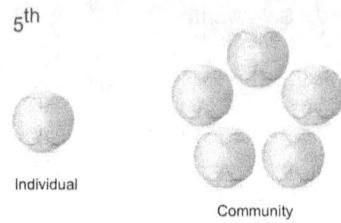

In the 1970s, I was one of the first female white-water river guides. But, to be accepted in the all-male world of boatmen, I had to prove my worth. To do that, I learned to read the water and transform my fear.

As I approach enormous rapids, a wall of fear arises that almost leaves me paralyzed. But, over time, I discovered how to transform the fear and place it behind me, giving me the power to guide my boat through the gigantic, thundering, life-eating rapids with elegant finesse.

The water becomes silky smooth at the top of a rapid right before it cascades down a narrow path. The bigger the rapid, the deeper the powerful undercurrent. The top of the water feels like silken glass; underneath, torrents surge, rumbling along the riverbed. It's the most glorious feeling to connect to the deep, raging undercurrent and, at the same time, feel the bottom of my boat floating on the smooth satin iridescent water.

Once in a while, as I put my oar in the river at the top of a rapid, the glistening water, the oar, my hand, body, river, and boat are all one; one unit, one being, one movement.

The Inner (R)Evolution:

Time stands still.

There is infinite opportunity to maneuver my boat—droplets of glistening water cascade on the edge of my oar. Oars swirl, full body pressure, the boat turns, gliding through the rapids. Each move is filled with perfection and grace.

There is no separate I; everything merges as one.

A transcendent moment ripples out as everyone on the river trip feels this opening of the space-time continuum, the union of different levels of reality, and the connection to the flow of all that is.

At the bottom of the rapids, passengers and people viewing from shore asked, "What happened?" Everyone experiences transcendence, an extraordinary moment where time stands still. Peeking through the veil of duality, everyone connects to the oneness of all that is.

The 5th dimension is where we begin to bridge beyond space and time into more subtle unseen magical elements. You've had those moments, perhaps fleeting glances when you feel a part of all that is. You become so expansive that you disperse into the infinite field of the cosmos. The inner knowing, the feeling of being connected to all that is, is profound.

We connect to all that is in various ways. For many people, this happens in nature or when they relate to animals. For example, Kathy Karn is an internationally acclaimed wildlife photographer and lover of elephants. Each time Kathy arrives in the wilds of Kenya, the elephants come for miles to greet her. The beautiful book, *The Wisdom of Elephants*[1], captures her connection with elephants.

In another example, Cathy Freeman is the first Australian Aboriginal person to win an individual Olympic Gold Medal. In the wonderful documentary, *Freeman*, Cathy recalls connecting with her ancestors during the race's final sprint; their energy supported her to a fantastic victory.

DR. CYNTHIA MILLER

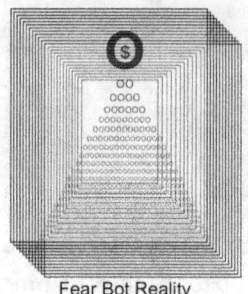
Fear Bot Reality

The Fear Bot cuts you off from your source and inflicts its rules and laws on your life. The 5th Fear Bot influencers are politics and governments. A mentality of separation, divide and conquer, us versus them, to keep people closed off from each other.

Colonization and the political war games of the Fear Bot govern and use authority to gain control, jurisdiction, and money, promoting separation and division to keep people in fear. The British Empire, at its height, ruled over a quarter of the world's population. Besides economic exploitation, the colonization involved human rights abuses and massacres.[2] It was the largest empire the world had ever seen, covering around a quarter of Earth's land surface and ruling over 458 million people.[3]

Governments strive for global governance, land, and command. The Fear Bot at play, peace is an illusion used to justify war, takeovers, and supremacy.

Since its beginnings in 1776, America has been at war 93% of the time. It's good for business, creates massive wealth for the few, and brings power and control.[4]

• Only three countries in the world America hasn't invaded or have never seen a U.S. military presence; Andorra, Bhutan, and Liechtenstein.[5]

• The United States has been militarily involved with 191 of 193 countries recognized by the United Nations, a whopping 98%.[6]

Governments create factions within their countries and against each other to keep people separated and cut off. In the US, the political parties wage war against each other while dastardly deeds occur. Unfortunately, the public is so concerned with the antics of the political parties that what's happening behind the scenes goes unnoticed or uncontrolled.

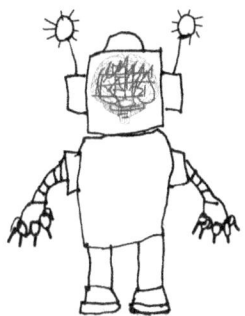

Political parties, influenced by bribes, lobbyists, and large donations, play into the deception game, while the voice of the majority is relegated to the background.
• The lobbying industry in 2021 used $3.7 billion to pressure Congress and the administration on how to allocate trillions of dollars in new pandemic spending and rules affecting health care, travel, tourism, and other industries.[7]

Governments and banks can cut you off at any moment because of their rules and regulations. For example, in 2022, as a means of control, Canadian bank cards of protesting citizens were blocked during the trucker's strike.[8]

The legal arm rules how you can live your life. The Fear Bot's tight grip on women is evident in laws that deny women's choice over their bodies. The right to access abortion care is essential for reproductive autonomy, social and economic equality, and the right to determine our future.
• Unwanted pregnancies, often due to rape or incest.
• Pregnancy complications that could result in the mother's death.
• Sexual and reproductive health and the rights of women to make their own decisions about their bodies are grounded in human rights to life, equality, privacy, and bodily integrity under international law.[9]

Since the US Supreme Court overturned *Roe v. Wade* and eliminated the constitutional right to abortion, many states have taken action to deny abortion care. Abortion is currently illegal in 12 states, and more states are expected to ban abortion in 2023.[10]

While abortion bans violate autonomy and bodily integrity, they also have deeply inequitable effects. Black women are three times more likely than white women to die from pregnancy-related causes.[11]

Women who miscarry face great risks, as it can be clinically difficult to distinguish pregnancy loss from attempted abortion. Providers could be required to report suspected abortions to law enforcement agencies, deterring women from seeking needed care.[12] Sweeping restrictions criminalize women and health workers, widen inequality, and increase deaths.[13]

Of course, there are many more examples of the Fear Bot in the 5th for you to explore.

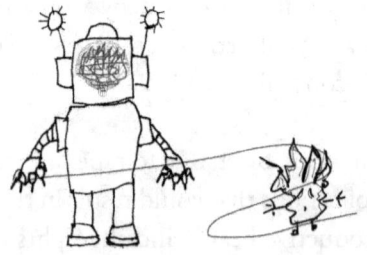

The Inner (R)Evolution:

When people conform to the mandates of the Fear Bot, they are easier to control, manipulate, and oppress. The Fear Bot laws of male supremacy preside over women; it's cheaper and less bothersome to command a docile flock of sheep than a group of powerful, free females.

The Fear Bot in the 5th cannot recognize the depth of who you are, so it tries to limit and squish you into a tiny box. Connected to your Childhood Circuitry, you feel alone, small, and disconnected—an imposter, muddled, unseen. Like a dark cloud, these underlying brain clamps and implants influence every part of your life.

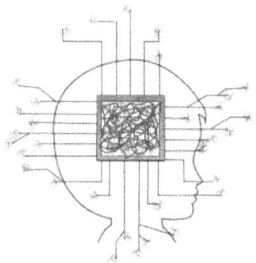

You lose touch with and are cut off from your authentic self. A tangled web, you're trapped, separate, and unconnected. On a deeper level, the corrupt DNA codes create a disconnection between you, your essence, and the more extraordinary expansive aspects of who you are.

We hide who we are, and the world sees the Fear Bot covered with the right clothes, makeup, and external trappings of success. All while trying to hide your true essence. Many of your connections with others are on the surface, consisting of small talk, chitchat, and gossip. You distort yourself to fit other people's expectations and perceptions of who you are supposed to be. You become a chameleon, shifting yourself for other people's benefit.

Your relationships are based on the false images you project to fit into the mold concocted by the Fear Bot. In a community, you morph yourself to conform, follow convention, and be accepted. Unfortunately, society is about herd mentality, fitting in, squishing who you are to adjust to the mass consciousness of the projection of who you're supposed to be—a fake human. As a result, you lose yourself.

As you join your 5th dimension with your Soul Circuitry, new inner freedom arises to be who you are. An internal relationship occurs with your expansive soul. The 5th is where the essence of you shines. All your outlandish, unique aspects are welcome, accepted, and honored. Rooted in your Soul Circuitry, the power of who you are is seen.

It's safe to come out of hiding in the new paradigm but not in the Fear Bot. So it's time to connect with your Soul Circuitry, see who you choose to share your precious life force energy with, and protect your energy. Do others receive your brilliant wisdom and cosmic knowledge with love and joy or with disarming fear?

Take a stand for who you want to have around you. The ones who inspire, ignite curiosity and fill you with laughter and fun. Those are your cohorts in creating a new reality. Experience the joy of your friend's quirky ways. Rather than trying to change them, enjoy their unique treasures and mysterious ways of seeing the world.

Many loners are craving community, not the old way of squishing ourselves to fit in with the crowd, but a new community of individuals, each eccentric in their unique way. Not someone to change, fix or control, but someone to have fun with and enjoy.

When you consciously change your inner landscape, your transmission alters, and friends and family notice the shift. You connect to a healthy ecosystem in your body, life, and the cosmos.

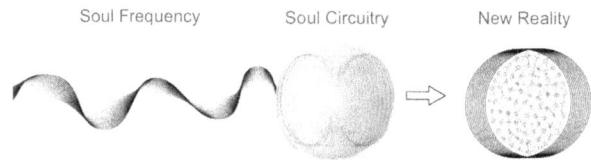

We are the Dream Builders here to create a new reality. So what's the new luscious reality? The grassroots movement starts within, reaching out to connect with others to share your gifts and incredible wisdom. Based on the highest values of love, gratitude, compassion, empathy, kindness, and generosity.

Break the cycle. Claim your individuality and your communities. Being in a community unlocks codes and a new level of integration and inner support. You feel held in love, part of a nurturing, loving community linked to the greater whole. We long for a community where we fit in, are seen, and are accepted.

What if it were up to you and some friends to create a new reality? What would you originate? We are evolving together, building as we go along. Each pod or community will be different.

How would a new type of community be organized? How can this unfold organically? What unique offerings do we each bring, and how can those be woven together to create something that's never existed before? Everyone will have different ideas and answers to these questions.

Establishing our communities in person in our neighborhoods and online globally is essential. Come together with groups of people in harmony with shared interests and diverse viewpoints. Share your brilliance and co-create a sustainable world.

One way is to start bringing more of your values to the town where you live. Then, when you and your neighbors join together, what exciting new changes do you want to make to create a safer community for everyone? What's your vision?

An unseen, grassroots movement is sprouting up around the world. People find each other. A global network operating on the frequency of love, mutual respect, and exchanging brilliant ideas with others to create a better world for all. As we each clean up our low-life Fear Bots and connect to deeper levels of our Higher Selves, the global networks strengthen, glistening shining brightly, exposing even more layers of the program.

Once started, it becomes a continuous process of awakening evolution. But we aren't at the critical mass yet.

We're creating a new luscious reality as a community event; we each have our strange, extraordinary, unconventional contributions and vision. A pixel in the grand tapestry of a new existence; without your piece, the image is incomplete. Each pixel informs others, spreading influence, and a ripple effect circles the globe. Ecstasy, love, and joy transmit through the quantum net, igniting luscious loving frequencies throughout the cosmos. We are the dancers co-creating the dance.

The 6th Dimension - AUTHORITY

An intense heartbreaking longing for spiritual connection pulled me to Tiruvannamalai, India, in 1994. It's the second day of Deepam, a festival dating back to 2500 BCE. According to legend, the Hindu deity Lord Shiva manifested as a column of light in the form of Mt. Arunachala. So, each year ghee, or clarified butter, is taken to the top of Mt. Arunachala and lit into a fire. Millions of people gather and walk an eight-mile pilgrimage around the Holy Fire Hill, Mt. Arunachala. Swarms of people chant, boom boxes blast, while pickpockets secretly steal their way through the crowds. Incense swirls and garlands of marigolds decorate altars along the way.

While crowds of people circumambulate Mt. Arunachala, I walk a deserted trail inhabited by raging monkeys that steal your food, deadly vipers, and cobras; only the brave, spiritual seekers make the trek alone. I'm sitting isolated in Sri Ramana Maharshi's meditation cave at Skanda Ashram. The cave is the size of a big bathtub carved into the heart of Mt. Arunachala. My bare palms and soles drink in Arunachala's fire. Then, in a flash, Shiva's luminosity ascends my body and flares out the top of my head. The surge of Shiva's fire ignites my Shakti.

Shiva and Shakti represent the divine union of consciousness and energy. From a metaphysical viewpoint, they are the two essential aspects of the One. The masculine principle, Shiva, represents the abiding aspect of God, and Shakti, the feminine principle, energy, life itself, and the act of creation.

I leave the cave and walk down the hill, disconnected from my body. I'm floating; my feet barely touch the ground. The squalid beggars look beautiful; even the filth and stench of excrement and rotting garbage turn into the luscious scent of jasmine. The plight of the beggars is irrelevant as I see beauty everywhere. The problems of the earth are trivial, unworthy of loving, focused attention.

The dirtiest, smelly, insect-infested places shift into a dazzling delight. The disgusting turns into awe, grace, and beauty. Radiance drenches everything. I exist in an illuminated state of ecstatic sublime, bliss, and gratitude. Everything is alive and pulsating, bathed in a luminous luster. From this vantage point, others' pain and suffering pale compared to my rapturous exhilaration.

I am out of my mind and body in nirvana, Satori, one-ness. I'm in a state beyond suffering, desire, and a sense of self. The state mystics write about divine rapture, an illuminated consciousness many long to achieve.

I become aware of a large disk about twelve inches above my head, denying me access to the angelic realms and higher dimensions. An energetic pathway, on my right side, at a 66-degree angle, steals my Shakti. A spiritual bypass, an energetic cut, siphoning off my energy into the Fear Bot. In exchange, I feel euphoric.

The Inner (R)Evolution:

The spiritual becomes more important than the physical, creating an imbalance, a top-heavy reality, disregarding the lower part of my body. As a result, I'm sucked into the grip of abandoning my precious essence for a heady, unsustainable state of nirvana. Seduced into the spiritual quest searching outside myself, I deny my soul connection.

I reach a self-absorbed state, the suffering of others beneath me at my feet. In many spiritual practices, we kiss the guru's feet. Bow down before him, prostrate ourselves—complete surrender, body, mind, and soul in exchange for an enraptured state of detached enchantment.

I want a full-body awakening. My path is not one of disconnection but of diving deep into the feminine mysteries residing in the lower part of my body. I long for a connection to my feminine essence. I miss my relationship with the angels.

The ecstasy and euphoria come at a very high price, the price of separation and cruelty. The problem is this spiritual awakening is partially out of my body. This tradition denies the body, making it less important than the spiritual. This practice, passed down for generations, continues today to feed the forces that keep violence, self-disrespect, and fear in motion.

I attain the pinnacle of spiritual seeking, only to discover it's not what I want. By the eighth day in this revered state, the novelty thoroughly explored, it becomes clear this awakening is not the answer to my internal search.

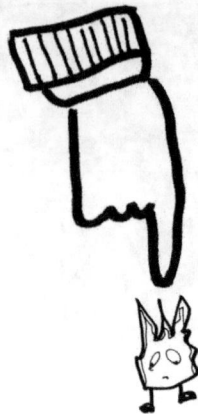

Religion reinforces the 6th dimension of the Fear Bot. The myth is that we are separate from source, and we need an intermediary, a man, a priest, or a religious leader as the go-between between God and us. Lost, we seek refuge in an external male authority; the Father knows best. An outside male dominance filters our mystical, spiritual experiences.

Religion is also a form of global control to create division, hatred, and war. My God is the Almighty, and I have the right to kill you if you don't follow my beliefs. If you don't believe in my God, you are inferior and a heathen sinner. My scriptures are the truth; yours are wrong. Maybe I can tolerate yours, but my religion is better, right, the only path.

A pyramid Ponzi scheme with the Father at the top and humanity slaving below to cater to his whims. Redemption through pain and suffering. Then, you reap the rewards in the next life in heaven. Life here is about toil, struggle, putting your nose to the grindstone, and cutting off your source connection with your body.

In the Fear Bot's model, you don't fit, so you either think something is wrong with you that needs fixing or that you've sinned; therefore, you need saving. An outside authority has the power, while you see yourself as a helpless victim of circumstance. The Fear Bot proclaims what is best for you. But the external forces act in their best interest, not yours; a mentality that promotes external control geared to manipulate your emotions and devalue your inner knowing.

• Religion in the United States is worth $1.2 trillion a year, making it equivalent to the 15th largest national economy in the world.[14]

• The faith economy has a higher value than the combined revenues of the top 10 technology companies in the U.S., including Apple, Amazon, and Google.[15]

The Fear Bot financiers on the 6th dimension are the religions that set up lies about our sinful nature and then demand money for forgiveness and redemption—a crooked, corrupt, convoluted system designed to keep us subservient.

We idolize the priest, ministers, and gurus who keep us in our place beneath them. Only a few reach this status; everyone else is lower, less spiritual, and less enlightened, so we give them our money.

• The Church of Jesus Christ of Latter-Day Saints: The church is among the wealthiest and richest churches in the world, commonly known as the LDS Church or the Mormon Church. **It is worth about $100 billion**.[16]

• The Catholic Church Vatican's national wealth is estimated to be $33 billion, Catholic Church Germany's -$26 billion, Catholic Church in Australia – $24 billion.[17]

The Fear Bot's been tampering with and playing with your soul since way back in time. According to the Papal Bull, "Unam Sanctam," the Roman Catholic Pope has supreme control over everyone's soul and body. Unam Sanctam ('One Holy'), the most famous papal document of the Middle Ages, affirms the pope's authority over all spiritual and temporal human powers.

For decades, Catholics were forbidden to use birth control. The church wanted to increase its population of followers to receive more souls, donations, and money—massive control over all aspects of your life, body, and soul.

Confess your sins, and you'll be fine. The priest voyeur hiding behind the curtain, the sinner's stories turn him on, tantalizing excitement all while making the person wrong. The pious priest, who preaches sin and redemption, sleuths around in the dark recesses of the church and rapes altar boys and innocent teenage girls. A corrupt system of male supremacy mixed with religion. The same thing happens in all religions.

The Fear Bot uses the low frequencies of blame, shame, and guilt to exploit people and keep them small and lifeless while siphoning off their life force. It's a tactic to drain our energy.

For example, when a man rapes a woman, she is criticized. This system blames, stigmatizes, and humiliates the women men have raped. Shamed, she carries profound guilt—the whole process triggered by some raging dick who doesn't know how to grow up. The women are made wrong; the men keep getting away with it.

- For every 1000 rapes in the US, 995 perpetrators will go unpunished.[18]

According to this twisted dogma, the woman's nature is sinful. Therefore, she has no means of redemption. To redeem herself, she has to be a virgin and give birth to a boy. Then she's OK. Her only purpose in life is to continue the male lineage.

Your job is to repent, prostrate to God, and give the religious authority enough money, so he'll pray for your sick soul. Make yourself small, a lowly sinner in the eyes of God. Your soul is forgiven with enough penance, bowing down, and financial donations until you take your next breath and sin again.

We give authority over our soul to some external priest or minister; they are supposed to know more than we do. But how can someone know your soul better than you? That's impossible. Your soul is the deepest essence of who you are, your magnificence. That scares religions; you'll find your inner freedom and leave them penniless and powerless.

The Inner (R)Evolution:

Your soul essence doesn't belong to some long-haired, bearded dude sitting on a throne in the sky, surrounded by naked cherubs. No separate, required outside authority, no middleman to pay a bribe to get you closer to source.

Why do you need a priest, minister, or guru when the divine creates life in your womb? Your soul essence is yours. You are source. Source is within you, a part of every cell of your body.

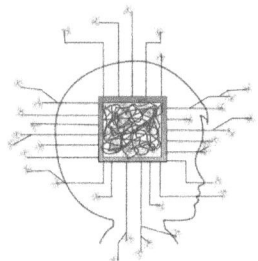

When in your Childhood Circuitry, you distrust yourself and have little or no confidence in what you know. Direct contact with your soul is cut back, pruned, and chopped out. You develop a dependence on others to show the way. Doubt, disbelief, uncertainty, and mistrust eat your inner wisdom. You swallow lies regardless of how your body responds. Depression and anxiety grow.

The low frequencies of shame, guilt and blame take over. Distraught, you plunge into the self-destructive pit of disgrace and dishonor. A perpetual loop keeps you feeling like a scum while supporting a system that degrades and humiliates you.

Your connection to source is denied; you believe you connect to the divine through the top of your head. This connection is to outer male authority, which uses your feminine energy to support the Fear Bot reality system.

The Fear Bot is the mentality of martyrs, self-deprivation, where others come first. With the suffering and the burden, you can't rise to your full potential when you carry the world's weight on your shoulders. You have to suffer for the greater good, and as a consequence, the current reality continues.

Another aspect of the 6th Fear Bot is spiritual bypass. Fleeing out the top of your head feeds the system you are trying to escape. Trying to leave out the top of your head, pretending the decaying structure doesn't exist, and living in a world of fake white light cut off from the lower part of the body—an attempt to evade the cruelty of the world and circumvent the wiring in your body. The lower part of the body is left behind, unprotected; the Nasties descend and suck up your feminine life force.

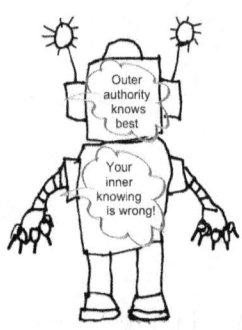

In the Fear Bot on the 6th dimension, external authority is more important and carries more weight than inner knowing. You squish yourself down to fit in; the outer rule is more potent than trusting your guts. You make yourself smaller so the external authority can suck your energy to inflate his insatiable ego. The child bully feeds everyone's fears to support his greedy, killing, raping sickness. Yet we all are providing the system with our unconscious energy.

We are lowly sinners, so we must follow the dictates of those in the know to save our souls and be released from perpetual damnation. So we beat ourselves up or try to fix ourselves, root out the sinner, the devil, that lurks within our body. When we hear something enough times, it becomes perceived as the truth, the spiritual law.

The sinner and the devil are the Fear Bot, not your essence.

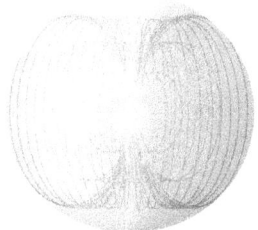

Disconnect from outer authority and reconnect to your Soul Circuitry, the essence of you. Invite your soul frequency on the 6th to fill your body. The expanse of your inner authority and power grows. Trust your gut and inner knowing, and connect with your divine soul essence. This aspect of you brings profound gifts, inner wisdom, and knowledge.

Reconnect to the divinity within your body. Claim your inner knowing. You are discovering your values and beliefs and claiming more significant aspects of your inner knowing. To move forward to create your unique, joyous reality, it's essential that you trust your internal wisdom.

It is a courageous leap to trust your inner knowing rather than digesting spoon-fed lies. Instead, look to and count on your soul, the divinity that is you, in alignment with your values and truth. We are forging a new path, claiming our bodies, minds, and souls for our awakening and evolution. Trusting your inner knowing is the key to the new reality.

>   Your soul is yours.
>   Your body is yours.
>   Your neurology is yours.

> Your DNA is yours.
> Take ownership.
> Stand up for what you believe.

Radiant flow tickles; a smile broadens. Happy, divine ecstasy surges. Exquisite luxury, embodying all of you, a delicious homecoming. Inner healing and contentment beyond your wildest imagination, tingling aliveness.

Happiness, wholeness, resting within, complete, no more searching; an exquisite excitement arises. Claim your inner authority, receive your power, and create a new reality. Rather than being pushed forward by fear, invite pleasure and joy to lead the way.

The 7th Dimension - CREATIVITY

After trekking in the remote Himalayas for three months in 1976, I was curious to see what was happening in the world. I was the assistant leader on the first Mount Everest clean-up expedition. We trekked up to 18,500' and picked up trash from forty-three countries. And then, for two more months, surrounded by the planet's highest peaks, I journeyed through a magical landscape beyond the media and consumerism culture. The day before my visa expired, I left Nepal.

At the airport in New Delhi, India, I bought the Asian edition of an American weekly magazine. In Rome, I bought the European edition of the same magazine. Finally, in New York, I purchased the American

The Inner (R)Evolution:

version. Twelve flights, seventy-two hours from Kathmandu, Nepal, to San Francisco, California; I read all three magazines cover to cover. I was shocked to read about world events from three unique perspectives and became aware of the media's manipulation of global reality.

The magazines came out the same week, carefully curated, each with a different viewpoint to believe, so we fear, hate, and distrust people in other parts of the world. Before the age of the Internet and instant global connection, I became aware of how American news engineers and manipulates global reality.

Unfortunately, I had no idea how to discern the lies from the truth. This was 1976, before the Internet; since then, the lies have become more sophisticated.

Having lived in India, Switzerland, Iran, and the US, I was aware of the cultural mindset of each magazine edition. As a result, I could readily see how the news fit into and helped shape the view of reality for each global region.

The Fear Bot uses manipulative advertising, propaganda, and brainwashing to create our current reality, pawns in a game constructed to make you feel like a helpless victim while cutting off creativity. The Fear Bot, built on lies, creates a false reality we are programmed to believe.

The tentacles of the Fear Bot in the 7th manipulate your core. Advertisers use unscrupulous ways to wrangle our brains to contort to their thinking.

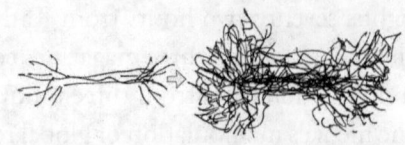

Corporations and governments use advertising to feed our brains. So over time, our neurons shift. The repetition becomes wired inside; the bundle increases each time the nerves fire.

Repeatedly exposing your subconscious to bad stuff is especially dangerous as repetition influences your mind even more intensely. Your subconscious makes you do things on autopilot.

• Digital marketing experts estimate that most Americans are exposed to around **4,000 to 10,000 ads each day**.[19]

We listen to the news, masterfully created by the media, intensifying anxiety, fear, and inner horror, causing increased blood pressure, sleeplessness, and heart problems. The panic of the news becomes addictive. Then the prescription drug commercials sell you wonder drugs to relieve their fear-induced propaganda.

• Only two countries in the world allow for direct-to-consumer pharmaceutical advertising: the US and New Zealand.[20]

• In 2020, the pharmaceutical industry in the US spent $4.58 billion on advertising on national TV.[21]

• In 2020 TV ad spending of the pharma industry accounted for 75% of the total ad spent.[22]

Profit is the mission of the corporation. So, mind manipulation of the masses to make them buy is a primary interest. Brainwashing is more important than the workers' lives. The workers are expendable. Creating loyal, life-long customers is essential to keep receiving massive profits.

- World's Largest Advertisers In 2021:[23]
- 1. Procter & Gamble, Annual Ad Spent: $11.5 Billion
- 2. Amazon, Annual Ad Spent: $10.9 Billion
- 3. L'Oreal, Annual Ad Spent: $9.9 Billion
- 4. Samsung Electronics Co, Annual Ad Spent: $8.6 Billion.

The new normal of tailored advertising means that big tech will monetize your online habits — and your privacy.

Amazon has a new program where select customers can use an app to submit photos of receipts for ten bucks, complete surveys for cash — and most invasively of all, allow the app to spy on your phone's traffic.

- Amazon says it'll pay you $2 per month to spy on your phone's internet traffic.[24]

Advertisers have begun invading our sleep to place their products in our dreams to shift our purchasing through dream hacking. The media isn't dumb; they know the subconscious picks up messages and takes them on as the truth.

- Multiple marketing studies are testing new ways to alter and drive purchasing behavior through sleep and dream hacking. The commercial, for-profit use of dream incubation — presenting stimuli before or during sleep to affect dream content — is rapidly becoming a reality.[25]
- A trio of researchers at Harvard, MIT, and the University of Montreal published an essay on dream hacking, warning that, according to a recent survey, 77% of marketers plan to use dreamtech advertising in the next three years.[26]

It's only a matter of time before tech companies that make watches, wearables, apps, and other technology that monitor our sleep start to sell that data for profit or use those tools to hack our dreams while we slumber. Worst of all, you probably won't even remember it.[27]

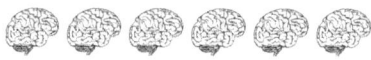

The contrived picture of reality is presented to us a gazillion times a day, creating a fake consumer reality. With enough exposure, we begin to believe the lies. Social media is a prime example.

• From 2020 to 2025, the number of people worldwide who use social media is expected to grow from 3.6 billion to 4.4 billion. That's over half of the entire planet's population scrolling through social feeds.[28]

Social media brainwashes you into believing a picture of a fake reality—designed to make you think and act in specific ways, how to spend your money, and where to focus your life energy.

Have you noticed you can do a google search, and a few minutes later, it shows up as advertising on your Instagram feed?

• Ad spending on social media is projected to reach over $173 billion in 2022.[29]

• Studies show links between smartphone usage and increased levels of anxiety and depression, poor sleep quality, and increased risk of car injury or death.[30]

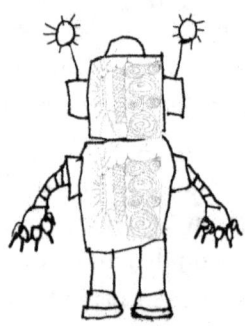

The Fear Bot on the 7th is where marketing and advertising exist, cheating Veils of Illusion. The media's ally is fear, designed to make us believe and act in specific ways, how to spend our money, and where to focus our life energy.

The hidden deceptive energies pull the global strings. The secret agenda, the closed-door policy, and the cover-up news are geared to trigger our fear, sympathy, and emotions in alignment with the propaganda machine on the 7th. Meanwhile, behind the curtain, The Fear Bots' allies are cooking up another scheme to keep people in servitude.

We are fed propaganda to consume. We are led to believe that if we buy the right products, our needs will be satisfied. When we have a great car and use the right shampoo, we will be loved and appreciated. Consumption solves all our problems. Advertising manipulates us to buy toxic junk to fill the gaping hole inside. The trauma deepens—a merry-go-round designed to amass great wealth for the few.

Fear disables the higher brain functions, and the brain is receptive to manipulation, false information, and mind control. In addition, the brain on fear triggers responses based on brainwashed propaganda.

Media and propaganda help create the Veils of Illusion, a counterfeit worldview. With enough advertising, we start to believe the myth. We're supposed to live in a fairytale, but most of us are the little minions running around so a few billionaires can lead their fantasy lives. So we turn to outside authority, the advertisers, to show us the life we want. It's a perfectly engineered nightmare that creates unnecessary wants while focusing on profits.

We are bombarded daily with fake news; we don't know how to distinguish flimflam from reality. The subconscious can't differentiate between reality and imagination. As a result, culture and society become sicker, more twisted, and distorted—a polluted system run by the Fear Bots—seven-year-old grown-ups. The pandemic has exacerbated a divide, who do we trust, what is accurate, and what is true—all creating an uproar of animosity, hatred, and fear. The programmed lies are so deep in our bodies that it's hard to discern the truth.

I just had my birthday; I'm seventy-seven, and I notice that my body is shutting down. Over the past few days, my knees have been on fire; I can barely wobble up and down the stairs using handrails and walls to support me. I hit panic mode; oh no, do I have to go to the doctor and get some pills? I'm scared this will get worse if I wait. My initial panic sends me to search outside myself for help.

Then I look around at the advertising, and the Veils of Illusion that create an overlay of aging and getting old, being decrepit, needing a nursing home, taking lots of meds, and living a restricted life in an elderly community. All ways to steal my money, rob me into the grave. Each year another blanket of lies covers my psyche. It's almost impossible to move; it looks like external wires drill deep into my nervous system and cellular instructions. I journey within and, using Light Codes, release the Veils of Illusion. The fire in my knees recedes, and new vitality fills my body.

How much of our sickness, aches, and pains are programmed by the media? Our cells and unconscious pick up and listen to the 4,000 to 10,000 ads we receive daily and use that programming to influence our bodies.

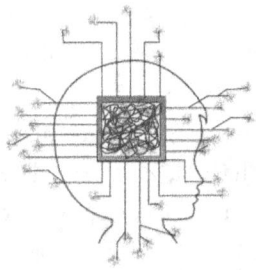

When you are run by your Childhood Circuitry, you believe the media's propaganda about which country is the enemy, which house and car will make you happy, and which pill will fix you. You try to keep up with the force-fed reality by purchasing the right stuff. When caught up in consumer buying frenzies, deep inner torment builds. But that leaves a gaping, empty hole. You begin to accept the fake, manipulated reality as the truth, so you judge your creativity since it doesn't look like the image presented. As a result, you feel riddled with self-doubt and inner criticism.

The starving, tormented artist syndrome is a prime example of the Childhood Circuitry interfering with creativity. Many creative souls are aware of the twisted and distorted energies of the Fear Bot. Our creativity is frivolous, a hobby to be pursued on the side while we do "real work" that keeps the Fear Bot moving forward.

Being in the creative flow is an exquisite part of being human. But, the mind tells us it's useless; it doesn't fit in with the majority. When your creativity is bashed, ridiculed, and made wrong, it's like being punched in the core. The negativity makes you judge your creativity.

Confusion arises. How to separate what you want from what everybody else has told you you're supposed to want? Everybody else's desires are woven into your nervous system early on and wired into your Childhood Circuitry. And daily, you are bombarded with advertising and messages about what you're supposed to have to be accepted, fit in, and succeed.

Creativity was my response to fear and pain, create or die. At times I got so frantic inside that it felt like I'd die if I didn't design something, a temporary respite from internal torture. But I was stuck criticizing and judging my creations rather than loving and honoring them. Wreckage, strewn by the wayside, I ignored the force behind my designs, passing it off as child's play, of no consequence. Since I didn't value my creativity, it was hard for others to see its worth.

We squish our weird creativity. It doesn't look like anyone else's, so we judge it, compare it to others, and make ourselves wrong. As a result, we believe our creations, vision, and world view is wrong; it doesn't fit the picture presented in the media. We question our true heart desires rather than examine the neural circuitry that directs our thinking. As a result, our creativity gets reduced to support the Fear Bot rather than our soul.

We are programmed to squelch our souls' vision and listen to the brainwashing that tells us we are crazy to desire our natural state. But then, we get curious and listen to the almost silent whispers, glimpses that there is something better. When we start seeing the depth of the insanity, it's shocking.

How do you choose to use your creative life force? To create junk for people to consume or provide nourishment for the heart and soul? Connect to your Soul Circuitry. Your weird vision, unique ideas, and strange worldview are needed—your brilliant imagination, passion, and gift to raise consciousness and humanity's frequency. The solution, trust your guts, creativity, imagination, and dreams; that's the actual, magical reality.

The Inner (R)Evolution:

Play with Light Codes to dissolve the Fear Bots. Surround the advertising with Light Codes. Draw them, doodle, find the hidden gems, and bring them to the light of day. Start a journal, use your creativity to discover your core values underneath mind manipulation, advertising, TV, news, and social media.

Your creativity will help you escape the absurdity of the world. Creativity is the expression of your soul's essence. Your soul signature is manifesting on earth. We all are creative; everyone is different.

The higher frequencies of the 7th invite you to be creative and courageous to dream up your reality. When you are in the flow, you connect to source. Artists, authors, explorers, musicians, actors, leaders, coaches, change-makers, and the list goes on, exposing us to their worlds and their vision of reality. We each live in our reality bubble, so why not create one that fills your heart, makes you sing and dance for joy?

What gifts of your creativity do you choose to share? The 7th is the dimension of business marketing, creating your brand, and communicating the message that only you can share. The world needs your weirdness. Be bold, courageous, and creative. What's your vision for your life and humanity's future? It starts with you and the difference only you can make.

Allow your soul essence to reveal itself. I had an art teacher who said, "What you paint is none of your business; it's your soul's expression." Judgment, self-doubt, and comparison to others inhibit your divine essence flow.

You are unique; you have the power to let your genius out of the box. The challenge is trusting your instincts and creating something only you can make. It won't look like anyone else. Exposed, share your secret gifts with the right people, and create a magical reality.

How will you use your new vision and luscious inner life to create an external reality where everyone can flourish? What kind of reality do you want to birth?

Your Soul Circuitry on the 7th creates your vision of a beautiful world for all, your dream filled with joy, love, sharing, and connection. The deepest desires of your heart, connected with your magnificent creativity and unique contribution, create a new reality. The new world comes to life in a community; a few at the top do not make it.

You've had moments of being in the flow, connected to soul essence, beyond time, hours flying by. You have a specific contribution—your vision, passion, and pleasure, like no other. What brings you joy is your creative essence. Create your art form, transform your life and business, and add your one-of-a-kind twist.

Change from living other people's dreams to envisioning your magical life.

Claim and celebrate your creative power!

The 8th Dimension - SELF-WORTH and VALUE

In 2006, I embarked on an exciting adventure to find a new home and move into the next phase of my life. I sold my house, stored my belongings, and ventured on a fun road trip to the high Rocky Mountains in Colorado. Emerging from the wilderness, I'm horrified. My life savings, profits from the sale of my home, and retirement are all lost in the stock market. And somebody stole almost everything I own from the storage company.

In the flash of a stock market scandal, I'm a bag lady, pushing my cart through the discounted aisles in the grocery store, rummaging around and in the dumpster for food, and racking up my credit card bill. The Ph.D. that had experienced a thriving practice changing people's lives feels like an imposter, a charade. The despicable, unworthy, wretched me must be the real me. I'm penniless and worthless; therefore, I have no value.

The desperation of being homeless, destitute, and with no money at sixty is overwhelming. Terror fills my body. I'm despicable beyond social acceptance.

No one wants to associate with a homeless bag lady. Look the other way, pretend she doesn't exist, cross the street, so you don't have to walk by her, slumped over in tattered jeans, hugging her knees, rocking in a fetal position, babbling.

In the privacy of my tent, I howl to the woods and sob into the ground; the sanctity of mother earth holds me. Alone in bear country, I'm camped near a town where I know no one, and when I meet people, I'm not about to tell them I'm an impoverished bag lady.

The weight of guilt and shame of my existence crushes my ability to function. The stigma I carry of my father's legacy runs deep, beyond mental constructs, into my unconscious and DNA. My dad's dirty money was gained from annihilating large populations of select people, destroying the ecosystem, and spewing toxic radiation around the world. Dirty money from the Fear Bot feeds war, violence, and corruption. I want nothing to do with it.

The dirty money from my inheritance is mixed in with my life savings. My mind decides that I am the one at fault. The stock market scandal isn't important; I am a person of no value. Since I have no money, I have proof of my unworthiness. My self-confidence disappears; my dreams vanish.

Flames creep up my spine. My body quivers. I know I have my hand in creating this mess, but lost in the vast unknown; I can't see my way out. I'm confused about what is me and what is the toxic goo of the Fear Bot. I want to kill the inner tormentors, but I can't sort out the Fear Bot from my Self; since it's so embedded in my body, suicide feels like my only option.

I've contemplated suicide for decades, an unspoken voice hiding in my brain, lurking in my subconscious, wrapped around my DNA. I've been chewing on the details of my demise for years. Suicide, a taboo topic, is not open for discussion or inquiry.

A lifetime of pain is too much to bear. I don't want to be rescued or found. I don't want to leave a mess for someone else to clean up. I made my plan. Everything I need is in the trunk of my car.

The final preparations are underway; today is the day to end the horrors of this life. But, as I get into my car, a deep rumbling voice erupts from my gut, "Choose gratitude."

What do I have to be thankful for? My brain and guts are debating, more like a screaming match.

My guts bellow, "Choose gratitude."

My mind insists, "Be done, complete, end the pain; I've had enough." Nasties scream in my head about how worthless and second-rate I am.

My mother's words rattle in my brain, confirming the Nasties, "Who the hell do you think you are?"

After an inner argument, I commit to choosing gratitude, no matter what.

Gratitude came along, saving me from the pit of self-annihilation –a radical approach, thanking the pain, suffering, and inner torment.

That's the dramatic way I learned about gratitude. A much easier, gentler way to discover the depths of gratitude is to read my book, *The Art of Radical Gratitude*.[31]

Money and the Fear Bot play out in the 8th dimension in the banking and financial sectors. Money is the highest commodity, much more revered than your life and dreams.

The ultimate goal is to amass enormous wealth. Everything has one focus, create wealth for the elite, no matter the cost of human dignity and basic survival. Feed them crumbs and work them to the bone. Keep them alive long enough to squeeze as much money and labor out of people as possible—the age-old tradition of underpaying people based on the color of their skin and gender.

The imprinted inferiority of women created by the Fear Bot reigns worldwide. In many cultures and businesses, the woman's worth and value come through a man, father, husband, or boss. As a woman, you are worth less and paid less than men.

- Native American women earn $0.58 for every dollar, and Latina women earn $0.53 for every dollar earned by their white male counterparts.[32]

• Black women earn $0.61 for every dollar earned by their white male counterparts.[33]

• White women and Asian women earn $0.77 and $0.85, respectively.[34]

• In another report, in the United States, women earn as little as 49 cents on the dollar compared to men.[35]

Then there is the wealth gap.

• Women only own about 32 cents for every dollar of wealth owned by their male counterparts.[36]

• This gap is far more acute for black and Latina women.[37]

The insanity of the current reality continues.

• A Walmart associate in the U.S. makes about 6 cents, while the Walton's make $70,000 in the same amount of time.[38]

• The Walton's fortune of Walmart increases by $4 million per hour, $100 million per day.[39]

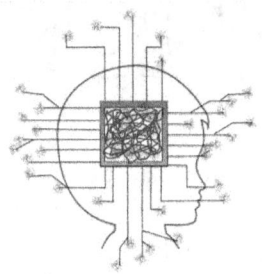

We're living in the propaganda machine's fabricated illusion that we must keep consuming. A shopping orgy, spending money we don't have on stuff we don't want, to impress others. Connected to your Childhood Circuitry, you are wired to believe your value and self-worth are related to what you own. An inner frenzy mounts; you must buy more junk to quell the internal panic, torment, and gnawing. You rationalize that after the next promotion, sale, or breakthrough, you will pay for everything you're buying on credit.

Banks reported blockbuster 2019 profits with the help of consumers' credit card debt.

The Inner (R)Evolution:

• Credit card debt hit a record high of $930 billion for Americans in the final quarter of 2019.[40]

The biggest industry in the world in 2021 is financial services, with a market value of *$22.5 trillion*.[41] Based on more consumption, the Fear Bot's economy is unsustainable and leads to massive wealth.

• In 2018, the global banking industry cashed in over $1.36 trillion in after-tax profit.[42]

The Fear Bot's money system perpetuates the scam of feeling unworthy, flawed, and not good enough— ingrained in your nervous system and rampant in the collective unconscious. In the Fear Bot, you have little or no value; you are an easily replaced cog in the current reality. Your only value is your net worth.

All the humongous numbers of wealthy Fear Bot-driven people are overwhelming. In part designed by the media to make you feel insignificant, worthless, and you don't matter. We are trained to believe we can be thrown away in an instant by corporate layoffs, a stock market heist, or a pandemic.

The mottos are the end justifies the means, and the bottom line is what matters. Profit at all costs to benefit the executives and shareholders. This mentality leads to slavery, appalling working conditions, and destruction of the environment, all for a quick almighty dollar.

• The globe's richest 1% own half the world's wealth.[49]

• The richest 1% bagged 82% of wealth created last year-the poorest half of humanity got nothing.[50]

• The 25 wealthiest family dynasties on the planet control $1.4 trillion.[51]

They added $312 billion to their collective fortunes, a 22% gain since last August.[52]

There are three myths used by the ultra-wealthy to justify their poverty-producing greediness.

1. The first is trickle-down economics. They claim their wealth trickles down to everyone else as they invest it and create jobs.[5] The rich move their businesses around the world to capitalize on paying the lowest wages possible to increase their profits. What trickles down is domination and control.

2. The second myth is the "free market." Robert Reich says, "In reality, the ultra-wealthy have rigged the so-called "free market" in America for their benefit. Tax cuts, freedom to bash unions and monopolize markets, and government bailouts. Their pockets have been further lined by privatization and deregulation."[43]

3. The third myth is that they're superior human beings — rugged individuals who "did it on their own" and therefore *deserve* their billions.[44] Most super-rich inherited their wealth or had upper-echelon connections that jump-started their businesses. They believe in a hierarchy where they are on the top, arrogant, entitled, and superior to others.

Chasing the dollar and the consumer lifestyle necessitates the need for more. There is never enough, no matter how much you have.

And here is another interesting tidbit. How can the government lose $21 trillion of your hard-earned tax dollars?

• $21 TRILLION of Pentagon financial transactions "could not be traced, documented, or explained."[45]

- The Federal Accounting Standards Advisory Board recommended that the government be allowed to misstate and move funds to hide expenditures if necessary for national security purposes.[46]
- The federal government will keep two sets of books, one modified (and useless) book for the public and one true book that is hidden. If the government is free to lie about what it's spending, it can also lie about how much it's borrowing.[47]

The Fear Bot's fake worldview creates a lopsided, skewed financial model of reality. We are programmed to hold those who have more money than us in high esteem. They are the super-gods we look up to and try to emulate. As the profit grows, the power increases.

- Eight billionaires — all men — have accumulated as much wealth as the poorest 3.6 billion people on the planet. They saw a 123% increase in their combined wealth, from $349 billion to $799 billion.[48]

Think about that, eight men's wealth relies upon the lives of 3.6 billion impoverished people without adequate food, housing, clean water, or healthcare. That is sick, insane money-grabbing power and control.

Women and girls put in 12.5 billion hours of unpaid care work every day — a contribution to the global economy of at least $10.8 trillion a year.[49]

How many millions of unpaid or underpaid women does it take to create one billionaire?

Think about that for a moment; females put in 12.5 billion hours of unpaid work every day. Women, where are you unpaid or underpaid? Keep noticing how and where you sell yourself short. Where do you shut down your power and clamp down your voice?

You are either creating your visions or someone else's. The question is, whose plans are you supporting with your conscious and unconscious life-force currency?

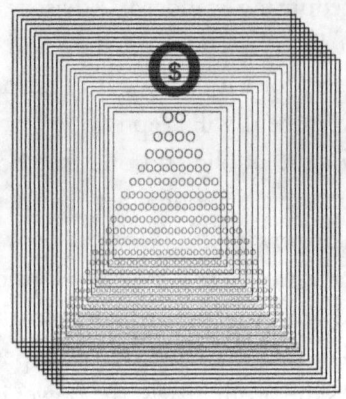

I've exposed a small tip of the money-life pyramid Ponzi scheme. It's obvious how the Fear Bot perpetuates the world's inequality, poverty, and fear. When you become curious about something, follow the money trail, and see what or who is pulling the strings behind the scenes. It's shocking to see the far-reaching implications of the Fear Bot.

You have power over your money. Does your spending take you closer or further away from the person you want to be? How you spend your currency daily tremendously impacts the world we create.

Diane Osgood's wonderful book, **Your Shopping Superpower,**[50] is an excellent guide to assist you in making wise shopping decisions that align with your values.

Move your money beliefs, philosophy, and values from your Childhood Circuitry and low-level Fear Bot to your Soul Circuitry. Give your money the freedom to evolve to manifest your desires in alignment with the ethics of your soul and heart.

The Inner (R)Evolution:

The lower frequencies of The Fear Bot on the 8th dimension foster feelings of unworthiness, being unacceptable, and inner poverty. When connected to the Childhood Circuitry, we buy into these lies, thinking something is wrong deep inside, that we are unworthy and so inadequate that we deserve all the hardships life throws our way. Our unworthiness then influences our ability to receive money, new possibilities, support, and other resources. We've left behind who we are. Each time we abandon ourselves, the lack of self-worth deepens.

The Fear Bot in your body creates unworthy neural programs and corrupt DNA codes, so no matter how many external accomplishments you achieve, you are never enough. The internal program that you are never enough is the Fear Bot.

It takes a good chunk of time to shovel your way through the Bottom Sludge and rewire the corroded, mangled, mashed-up wiring. It takes a while to sort it out and see what goes where. But your body knows the way.

The power of the Fear Bot is overwhelming. You feel insignificant, small, and worthless, just as the Fear Bot wants you to. That way, you will keep leading a mediocre life, working away. Once the Fear Bot drains your life force, you are retired. Your life force is exhausted, your body aches, and you lack motivation. You sit on the couch, watch TV and spend your money online. You keep taking more and more meds that eat up your life savings. Then the doctors and hospital bills devour every remaining penny you spent your life building. Your life is complete, in service to the Fear Bot, from birth to death. The Fear Bot defines your reality.

DR. CYNTHIA MILLER

"And gradually, though no one remembers exactly how it happened, the unthinkable becomes tolerable. And then acceptable. And then legal. And then applaudable."

- Joni Eareckson Tada

A SILENT KILLING, DRIP BY DRIP, DREAMS STOMPED ON, hopes dashed, a vision out of the norm diminished, made wrong—killing the human creative spirit, depression, hopelessness, and worthlessness set in. People's soul essence is squished into an outdated neural framework to benefit a few. The killing continues with contaminated food, toxic air, and polluted water, all outcomes of the Fear Bot mentality. This monster will kill us off. But we are the ones feeding the multinational corporations, the military machinery, and the pharmaceuticals. Everywhere we look, we see the degradation of our planet into a global dark state, ending in the extinction of humanity. We are at the point where it's do or die, sink, or swim. We are killing ourselves off in every dimension.

Take a deep breath. This information is intense—spiral love and gratitude around your body. Relax. Let go of the Fear Bot.

The Inner (R)Evolution:

Notice where you don't value yourself. See all the ways you short-change yourself. Selling yourself short enforces the fear program. Stand up for who you are and look your inner terror in the eye. Forgive yourself for your messy life. All the nasty parts of self-loathing. What would happen if you loved your past and your wounds, failures, and Nasties?

Create boundaries inside your body and choose where your unconscious energy flows. Decide where your conscious energy focuses and choose where to spend your money—claim your values, speak your truth. Manifesting your dream reality is based on your deepest essence.

Small steps add up to significant change. As you shift your consciousness and neural programming, that ripples out, creating greater global change and awakening. You are here to create a new world filled with love, compassion, and gratitude—where we all thrive in alignment with nature. Your manifested vision is essential to creating a new you and reality.

The 8th dimension is the Dream Builder, the realm of manifesting and living your dreams. Not the desires implanted in your brain by the Fear Bot but the deeply held goals and visions of your soul. But first, you need to value yourself. Then, it's necessary to have the resources and money to fund your dreams.

Your Soul Circuitry provides the internal structure to claim your worth. Remember, your neurology creates your reality. As you unplug from the Fear Bot, your life will change dramatically for the better. It requires courage and dedication, and the rewards are profound. The inner angst dissolves, and you feel fulfilled and complete. The frenzy to accumulate more junk doesn't run your life anymore. Profound contentment arises.

Break the cycle; claim your self-worth.

• Look closely, follow the money trail, and see where it leads. Then release the rage, anger, and terror in your body.

• My coloring book, *I Am Worthy*,[51] is a fabulous adjunct to further expand your worthiness's integration. So have fun, and color your inner transformation.

• Visit DrCynthiaMiller.com/checklists to download your free wealth matrix handout.

A NEW STORY OF VALUE, WORTHINESS, AND SUCCESS originates in your Soul Circuitry and essence, the role only you can play. Your Soul Self rewrites the script. An awakened level of consciousness. A never-ending process of expansion, evolution, and creation of a new reality. New possibilities open, your voice is heard, your message received, and your brilliance transmitted. Feel the power surge through your body as you stand for your beliefs.

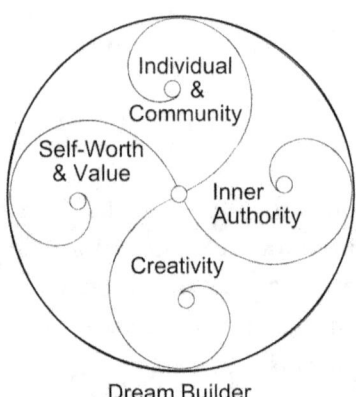

Dream Builder

Are you ready to embody your Dream Builder, the part of you that is here to envision a new you and a new world? The 8th inner architect reads your soul blueprint, mates with the other dimensions, and

The Inner (R)Evolution:

together, you build the foundation for your life. Follow your guts, inner guidance, and joyous pleasure.

Imagine being lovingly held in safety instead of pushing and struggling to prove your worthiness. Who you are is worthy and valuable, precisely as you are. Your Soul Circuitry embraces you, allowing your inner programs to transform safely—an ongoing process of conscious evolution.

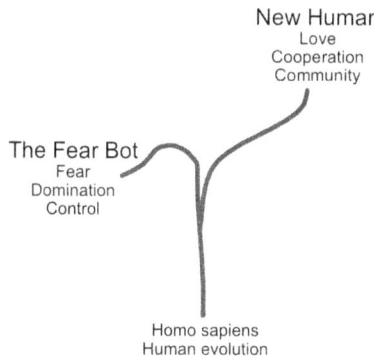

We are the Dream Builders, building a new reality. Considering humanity's time on earth, which is minuscule, we're at a big step. Humans are growing up beyond seven-year-olds. We can change how our nervous system and DNA function with our deliberate, conscious intention. A huge accomplishment, never available on a global scale before.

You're here to make a difference, or you wouldn't be reading this book. You are one of the courageous path-breakers on the cutting edge here to help manifest a new human and reality. So instead of re-creating your life for a better job and a bigger house, why not create an epic adventure?

What Dream Builder gifts and treasures do you bring to create your new story? It may take time to reveal the secrets. What magical archetype, character, or star lineage does your 8th Soul Self represent? The possibilities are endless. What unseen resources and magical connections are taking place beyond normal vision? The tapestry of life is fluid, ever connecting in mysterious ways.

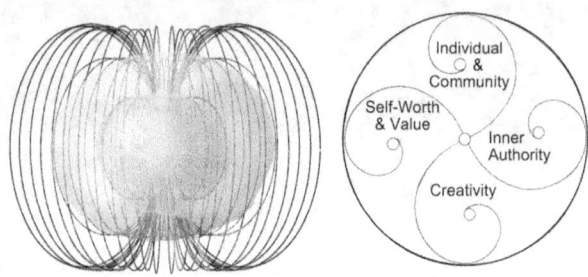

Dream Builder

Your 5th through 8th dimension Dream Builder Team creates the vision, money, resources, and connections to manifest your new reality. Not based on linear, left-brain concepts but designed with your unique creativity and inner authority. We are forging a new path, a community event creating a new reality.

Your Dream Builder Team brings bold, courageous qualities—an architect of your inner reality, manifesting in the outer world. The 5th embraces duality; we are separate individuals, and we are all connected. Retain your identity and unique creativity and be a part of a community. The 6th is claiming your inner authority, your wisdom, what you know is the truth for you—taking a stance, and standing up for what you believe. The 7th is vision, the creativity: your weirdness, voice, vision, and unique piece. Finally, the 8th is the architect, building the framework for your ideas, plus the money to fund your dreams.

Your Dream Builder Team is here, embodied in your Soul Circuitry. Your Dream Builder Team gathers, rewrites the play, architects your next evolutionary stage, and performs a magnificent act. The archetypal, galactic mythology of who you are, the bigger story that's playing behind the scenes. The character and role you play in the grander

The Inner (R)Evolution:

cosmic scheme. It's an exhilarating role to play. Embody your vast potential and possibilities, and embark on the adventure you've waited for lifetimes to explore.

> The future is the product of the decisions you make today.
> Unravel the greatest mystery of all, you.

8. INNER FREEDOM

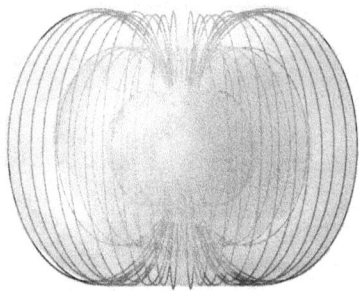

Inner Freedom, the 3ʳᴰ layer of the Soul Circuitry, holds your ability to embody all aspects of who you are, gain true freedom, and experience profound happiness.

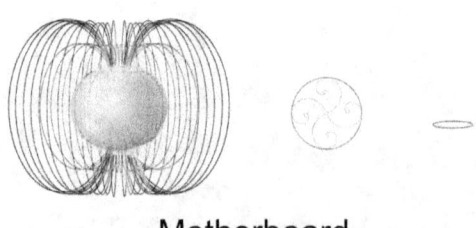

Motherboard

The Inner (R)Evolution:

EACH LAYER IS A PLATFORM THAT SUPPORTS YOUR evolution. We've seen that the first layer of the Soul Circuitry, the Motherboard, creates your magnificent, sustainable foundation. Trusting your life-force energy, being safe, loving yourself, and having strong boundaries are aspects of the Motherboard. The Motherboard is the rocket fuel; if it's not in alignment and connected, our dreams fizzle, derailed by the unconscious.

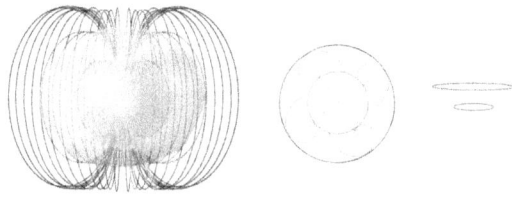

Dream Builder

The Dream Builder team is the architect of your inner reality, manifesting in the outer world. The 5th embraces duality; we are separate individuals, and we are all connected. The 6th is taking a stance and claiming your inner authority. The 7th is your unique creativity. The 8th is building the framework for your ideas, plus the resources to fund your dreams.

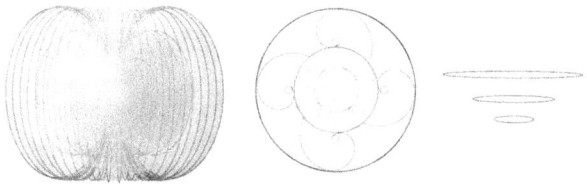

Inner Freedom

So, let's explore the third layer of the Soul Circuitry, your Inner

Freedom, expanded galactic energies, aligned masculine and feminine frequencies, and a greater connection to your higher amazing essence.

Emissaries from afar and near, past and future, earth and the vast cosmos, your multidimensional frequencies arrive from a vast array of places. Archetypes, goddesses, gods, dolphins, dragons, angels, mythologies, star families, galactic councils, animal spirits, or unicorns connect with your Soul Circuitry. The muse, mystical, and otherworldly aspects of your essence are accepted and integrated. The possibilities are endless; that's what makes it exciting and fun.

Which aspect of yourself relates to each dimension dramatically impacts your life. The plethora of diversity is staggering; we each have a vast assortment of gifts, talents, and knowledge to contribute. Explore your angel wings, magic wands, sparkles, voluptuous power, tantalizing delight, whatever your superpower.

The 9th Dimension - COSMIC AWARENESS

My initiation into the 9th was spectacular. It's only with hindsight that I put the pieces together and discovered what was happening.

Driving between Santa Fe and Taos, New Mexico, one snowy afternoon, I wind around the bend. At the bottom of the hill, a small bridge crosses the river. Two cars collide on the bridge, leaving no path to the canyon's other side.

My car's bald tires swerve on black ice. Snow is piled high on both

The Inner (R)Evolution:

sides of the road. Scared, I didn't know what to do. I flash back to all the miracles that occurred working with my clients and call on the angels for help. Eyes closed, hands lightly holding the steering wheel, one foot resting on the gas, the other on the brakes, I surrender. I keep calling on the angels. I use every drop of focus to be with the angels.

Deep in my inner wisdom, I know fear will envelop my brain and body if I open my eyes. I will be a pile of broken bones, spewing blood, shattered glass, and scrunched metal entangled with the two collided vehicles. But, if I keep my eyes shut, block out the fear, and retain a laser focus on my trust in the angels, somehow, a miracle will occur.

In a moment of space-time, the angels transport my car and me across the river to the other side of the canyon. My eyes still closed, I feel pressure on my foot on the gas pedal, and the car goes uphill. I open my eyes and, in the rearview mirror, see the awe on the faces of the people standing on the bridge. My car accelerates. I'm curious, wanting to know what the people saw, but I must keep going to the top of the hill.

FOR YEARS THIS EVENT REPLAYED IN MY MIND, TRYING TO figure out what had happened. Then, looking back, I drove my car across 9th dimension frequencies, angel wings, laid out like a freeway from one canyon wall to another, flying high over the river, bridge, and gaping canyon below. Beyond the ordinary, an extraordinary miraculous event. At that moment, I overcame the Fear Bot by remaining true to my inner self.

I've been flying, soaring through the cosmos, for as long as I can remember. My first memories were when I was two years old. Then, when I was four, I told my mother I flew with the angels every night. Her negative response was so intense I realized it was not safe to discuss. My dad built bombs and nuclear warfare; how could his daughter fly with the angels? That was forbidden territory, so I kept quiet.

I've been working with the angels with my clients for decades, and astonishing healings occur. A few people see my wings.

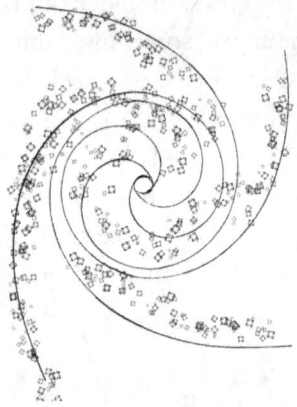

The 9th is an exciting dimension of your cosmic connection—a great place to re-examine your life story and how you see yourself. We're programmed to believe that we are limited to a 3-D body, cut off from our inner power and wisdom, a victim of circumstance. The 9th is where you can further expand into your vastness and connect with more unseen aspects of who you are.

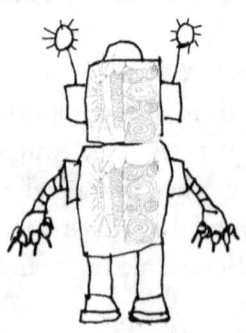

The Inner (R)Evolution:

The Fear Bot in the 9th perpetuates the belief that the cosmos is a hostile place, filled with strange beings with cruel energies ready to manipulate and take over humanity. But, beyond the Fear Bot, wondrous cosmic realities exist.

You try to fit in; you become invisible to become 'normal.' You worry about what others will think if they see the truth of who you are in other dimensions. Fit in the box, and cut out anything extraordinary, multidimensional, or cosmic. Limit your perception and knowledge of yourself to what is acceptable and presented by the media. Fear of being an outcast from an unknown place, a foreigner, an alien, conflicting with the status quo; so strange; it's terrifying. You deny all the weird, extraordinary things you know and experience. A split occurs, cutting off your mysterious magical powers.

Leave behind the shackles of the old paradigm that tie you down and keep you bound. Call on the Healing Angels to assist in releasing the Fear Bot. Their wings sweep out the old debris, and their high frequencies dissolve the Fear Bots, opening the space for your essence to shine.

What if all the stories of phoenixes, angels, star beings, gods, and goddesses are true? What if they are all aspects of who we are? We are so afraid of the ghoulish gremlins guarding the gate to our gifts that we deny our superpowers.

Long, long ago, gasses curled, asteroids and rocky planetoids collided, and the earth formed. You come from the stars; everything is composed of stardust, your galactic inheritance. Welcome to the 9th dimension, a magical connection to your deepest, most profound roots, swirling galaxies, celestial bodies of stars, and the Milky Way. We live on the most magnificent blue sphere, but we've lost contact with our roots, the earth, and the stars.

You've come from distant galaxies, far away star systems, and the deep reaches of the cosmos bearing gifts. Many of us, still cloaked in the Veils of Illusion, are the lightworkers, star seeds, multi-galactic beings, and grid workers. You are here from unknown galactic regions to assist with humanity's awakening and the evolution of consciousness.

You came in disguise, donned cloaks of forgetfulness, and joined the masquerade on earth. It's time to remove the veils. You are here in a body, pretending to be human. The only problem is your body is wired to the Fear Bot. Your brain and nervous system, stuck at the level of a seven-year-old, are trapped in a matrix of old paradigm consciousness.

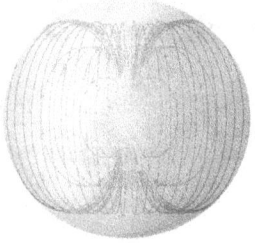

In your Soul Circuitry, you have a unique combination of where your galactic aspects fit into different dimensions. You know these aspects of yourself. You may have had glimpses, whispers, and inner knowing. Or you may know your cosmic friends better than most of your human friends. You are an emissary from a faraway galaxy, bearing wisdom, mysteries, and technologies.

Calling all angels, cosmic secret messengers, the ones who fly, soar, glide through the cosmos gathering galactic news; your luscious life-giving energy is safe. It's time to come out of hiding and create a new reality. Enjoy the orgasmic pleasure of birthing yourself into you. Claim your freedom, spread your wings, and soar. Connect to heaven and earth through your feet. The top of your head connects to the Fear Bot.

GET CURIOUS, EXPLORE WHO YOU ARE ON THE 9TH, AND CLAIM your superpowers. When connected to your Soul Circuitry, your hidden multidimensional wisdom and magic are seen, honored, and used to create your life and a new reality. Your life unfolds in magical ways.

The world needs your wisdom and wizardry.

The 10th Dimension - INNER MASCULINE

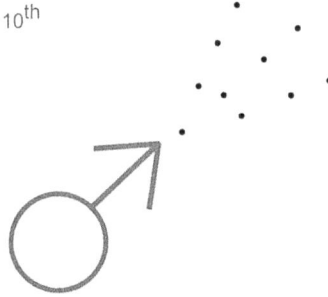

The 10th is a confusing dimension; it's so filled with patriarchy that it's challenging to uncover the healed divine masculine. The Fear Bot of the 10th holds the low frequencies of patriarchy, the degradation of women, and discrimination. The distorted masculine neural programs demand that the male is superior. Straight, unbending, rigid. Linear thought is in the highest demand; intuition and inner knowing are disregarded as fluff. The pattern goes so deep; sexism, racism, bigotry, homophobia, greed, and violence are all symptoms of manipulated neural programming. All of this is part of the Fear Bot on the 10th dimension that holds and keeps our lives captive.

Cut off from the inner feminine, the wounded male steals the feminine energy necessary for creation. A prime example is Napoleon Hill's money bible, *Think and Grow Rich, Chapter Eleven, The Mystery of Sex Transmutation*. Hill states, "It seemed quite significant to the author when he made the discovery that practically every great leader ... was a man whose achievements were largely inspired by a woman. In many instances, the **woman** was a **modest, self-denying wife**, of whom the public had heard little or nothing."

Nowhere does Hill discuss acknowledging the woman for providing the essential life-giving juice and power necessary for creations to manifest in the 3-D world. Only one can be on top in the hierarchy: the man and the Fear Bot game. The woman is always second-rate; however hard she tries, she's never good enough. Her life revolves around him, building the perfect backdrop so he is promoted, well-paid, and respected. He wouldn't be there without her, but he brushes her contributions aside as child's play. Instead, he uses her feminine essence to his advantage.

The arrogant belief that the woman's life-giving frequency is there for the man's taking, either sexually or energetically, to fuel the man's power and financial gain. Feminine energy is treated as a God-given right for the man to abduct, abuse, and use for his financial gain. It's been happening for generations. Abusing and raping women for the man's distorted pleasure and egoic status is part of the Fear Bot on the 10th.

- 81% of women have experienced sexual harassment.[1]
- Since the pandemic, these statistics have increased.[2]

- Every 68 seconds, an American woman is sexually assaulted.[3]
- In the US, over 1.5 million women were raped by an intimate partner in 2019.[4]

The Inner (R)Evolution:

The wounded masculine is emotionally unavailable, critical, and selfish; he needs to be correct; he is controlling, stuck in his mind, and afraid of failure. Many are in constant inner and outer conflict. The wounded male is enraged, pissed off, and angry, covering up how terrified he is—worried that he can't control the nature of reality.

The deranged masculine wants to fix, mold and shape women to fit his ideas. His arrogant dominion thinks he knows what's best. Frightened and suspicious that he's not powerful, he becomes aggressive. Then, like a schoolyard bully trying to prove himself, he builds himself up to gain outward approval and macho status, devoid of connections to his feelings.

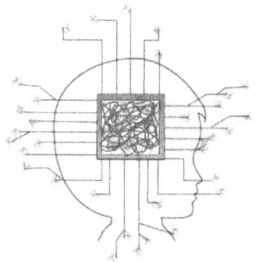

In the Childhood Circuitry, the inner feminine energies are cut off. Stealing feminine power for the man's gain is rampant, from sexual abuse to covert energy siphoning. Many men are oblivious to the depth of violation of the feminine. How many men have forced themselves on women, not listened to a woman's no, or taken things into their own hands?

The male's realization that he can't create and doesn't have the gift of life of the feminine promotes unconscious inferiority. The masculine response is to make the feminine wrong to build up his superiority and cover his feelings of inadequacy. So the masculine boosts his ego, puffs up his chest, and takes a stand.

The panic of the masculine is intense. The left brain has been in charge for eons. It's afraid to be taken over by the more significant force of the feminine. Linear logic is needed, but it's no longer number one. Fear takes over if the thought or energy goes beyond the realm of the left brain. The only acceptable reality is in the head.

The ultimate distorted male is cut off from his feminine energies. Feeling and emotions are the lower-class arenas of women. The last thing the mind wants is to let go and dive into the feminine, where it will drown in confusion until it figures out how to swim in the flow of the divine feminine.

It's too scary to venture out of the left brain into the belly and womb, forbidden taboo territory for the unhealed masculine. Your inner masculine has to confront what he does to your inner feminine. There's never a fair exchange; all he does is steal the feminine life-giving essence. So, the feminine shuts down, seals off, and hides to protect herself. The masculine predator will rape, kill, and devour her. Terrified, she cowers, hiding in the shadows.

The belief that the masculine leads the way is so deeply entrenched that it's burrowed in the base of your skull, wraps around your spine, and is in the center of your bones. Male dominance prevails, wired in your nervous system, passed down for generations, encoded in your corrupt DNA codes, creeping into every aspect of the unconscious. The brutal control of the masculine over the feminine has reached a point where men decide the laws and fate of a woman's uterus. Rage, anger, and frustration hold the Fear Bot in place.

The Inner (R)Evolution:

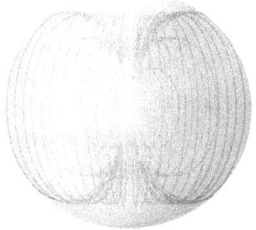

Your healed masculine on the 10th is the best friend, lover, and inner complement to your healed feminine on the 11th—the protective support of the masculine that listens and communicates in your most profound soul language. Your healed inner masculine provides boundaries and protection. Behind you, he has your back, with excellent safety and security. His arms wrap around the feminine, creating support, a structure to direct the feminine flow towards the intention, goal, and dream. Without the masculine, the feminine gushes everywhere, unfocused, and becomes watered down.

The feminine births the energy, and the masculine decides the direction. Remember, we have 40 million unconscious neural impulses per second. So where are you sending your unconscious energy?

The 10th healed inner masculine brings the direction, aims like an arrow, hits the bulls-eye, drives a point home, hits the mark, and forms structure. Creating the channel for your essence to flow like the banks of the river, guiding the flow of the curving wave cascading through your body, brings sacred nourishment to every cell. The masculine exposes us to the truth in a flash. Up and out, explodes in an instant, and spreads the seeds of his reality.

Give your healed inner masculine full permission to be in your body —an integral part of your life. He creates magnificent energetic boundaries, a safe environment, focused, full of integrity, and aligned with who you are. Not a straight linear path, your masculine Soul Self is wise, respectful, and listens; he knows how to create a fluid, changing pathway of safety that winds, curves, and spirals to accommodate the ever-changing feminine.

In the 10th dimension, connect to the lower part of your body and invite your masculine energy to flow all the way down to your feet. Allow yourself to feel the pleasure of your divine masculine. Start small. A daily practice of calling on your Light Codes, Spirals of Love and Gratitude, and the Fear Bot melts bit by bit. Over time the Veils of Illusion drop, and the insidious Fear Bot becomes more apparent. Each minor tweak ripples throughout your life and the world. Clarity emerges; disconnection from the Fear Bot is gradual as you build your new reality. You gain inner space, power, and grace. The ways you fed the Fear Bot drop away, leaving more energy and resources to fuel your dreams.

It's exquisite when you can trust your inner masculine energy after a lifetime of being scared, unsafe, and unprotected.

Start to explore who you are in the 10th dimension. What is your earthly, universal, or cosmic 10th connection that longs to be seen on earth? How can you love your inner masculine more today?

The 11th Dimension - INNER FEMININE

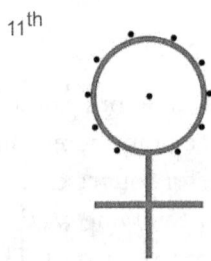

The Inner (R)Evolution:

With no warning, in 1973, I had a shocking, mysterious, radical initiation into the 11th dimension. A few days after surviving a near-death experience, I sat on the couch talking with my husband.

I'm suddenly aware of the consciousness in the cells in my left arm. In my next breath, a luminous bolt of energy shoots up from my tailbone, electrifies my spine, and explodes out the top of my head into outer space. My consciousness catapults out beyond ordinary reality. Incandescent air, colors appear brighter and fuller, having more depth and substance. Each cell is alive; each one is conscious—the wreckage of the massive energy bolt, a new brain configuration—all in one breath.

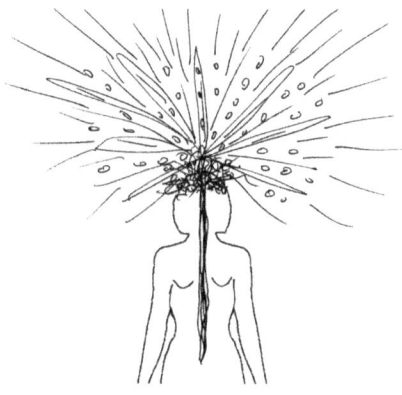

I look up, and I see inside my husband's body. Out the window, the trees display magnificent shimmering auras.

The shock of simultaneously seeing, knowing, feeling, and hearing multiple states of consciousness, some filled with love, others oozing terror, is unnerving, overwhelming, and sometimes frightening. I feel so alone. I have no one to talk to, nowhere to turn. It is too scary to speak of; my actions and the tiny bits I talk about are daunting to those around me.

The one thing I know for sure is to keep quiet.

For days I wait to return to ordinary consciousness. I finally realize there is no turning back. During the explosion out of the top of my head, a rearrangement took place. I can't return to the state I was in previously. Radical, permanent change, I'm propelled into other realms, with one foot still in 3-D reality. Numerous layers of stratum all jumbled together in one big unknown mess.

Beyond limited 3-D perception, my seeing is fluid, shifting between axons and dendrites, neurons bound together in patterns formed in early childhood trauma, floating into subatomic particles, and then flowing onto the angelic realms. As a result, my senses are rarified and intensified—a conglomeration of sensual input shifts throughout the day. At one moment, my vision changes, and the trees shimmer in iridescent colors, surrounded by golden halos; the colors of the grass intensify like the psychedelic paintings of the '60s.

About four years after this experience, a friend tells me she thought of me whenever she read the book, *Kundalini* by Gopi Krishna. Laid out in print, I read about everything I'm experiencing—wave upon wave of relief echoes through my body. I'm not crazy; I experienced a spontaneous kundalini awakening.

In Hindu and Tantric traditions, I discovered that kundalini is a form of divine feminine energy coiled up at the base of the spine. The released energy, known as Shakti, is the power of awakening, spiritual development, and evolutionary transformation.

Nowhere to turn; I'm without a rudder, a guide, or a map. I have to figure this out on my own. Shakti continues to surge through my body, reconstructing my life. To discover how I survived living with an unknown universe in my body, read my book, *Unseen Connections: A Memoir from Pain to Joy*.[5]

It's taken me years to sort through and unravel the dimensions and figure out what is what, like fitting together a cosmic multidimensional jigsaw puzzle. Five decades later, the seeing continues. Now, I've categorized dimensions and built this model, The Inner (R)Evolution, from my insights and working with thousands of clients.

Since my spontaneous kundalini awakening in 1973, Shakti, the feminine energy of transformation and evolution, has been an impressive, imposing force in my life. My 11th feminine travels and rides with the frequency of powerful, exquisite, all-consuming Shakti, mapping the path of transformation and evolution. Shakti is considered the cosmos itself.

The Inner (R)Evolution:

The wounded feminine on the 11th dimension is afraid to trust others, compromises her integrity and values, and is stuck in victimhood. Waiting to be saved, she drowns in her emotions and is manipulative. She feels unworthy and struggles with her self-image. Shame and insecurity add to her low self-worth. Afraid to speak her truth, she uses people pleasing to try to get her needs met.

The wounded feminine is compacted, like having a tight girdle around your spine and nervous system, held in place for eons, squishing the life out of you. Contain your energy and hold it in because it's too much if you let it out. The message is to constrain, restrain, and squish down your emotions, power, and energy. We're supposed to be nice little girls, docile, subservient, and mindless. The Childhood Circuitry molds the wounded feminine into various pre-made forms, trying to find the best fit. But none work; huge parts are left out, brushed aside, or forgotten.

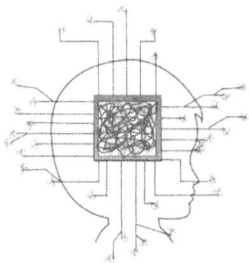

Breathing shuts down, so we don't take up too much space. Our bodies are wired to keep our feminine aspect closed up. Eons of trauma passed down for generations say that women are inferior and we better stick to our place. So, young lady, don't overstep your bounds. Who do you think you are?

Impacted in our muscles, flowing through our blood, packed in the back of the skull, deep in our bones, the low-frequency Fear Bot persists. It's so ingrained; that we don't know how to respond. It's the woman's duty, what we are born for, to produce offspring, mere cogs in the machine to keep the men on their omnipotent thrones. In many places worldwide, the woman's only purpose is to elevate men, have their babies, and be their servants. The woman, in herself, is worthless—this twisted reality permeates global consciousness.

The subservient female is the prescribed role dictated by the Fear Bot of how women function. The façade we are to put on to please the man, the boss, the father. For centuries, the woman's survival depended upon the man, so we donned the role of being second-rate. Women are crammed into a tiny box of who we should be. The wild, raw, emotional feminine essence denied gives way to the deranged, crazy, wrathful, wounded feminine.

Everything needs feminine energy to manifest. Unfortunately, the Fear Bot thrives on hijacking feminine power. Greedy patriarchs steal feminine energy to bring their plans to life, which leads to sexual abuse.

The impact of sexual abuse is profound. In my private practice, I worked with sexually abused women. Imagine a penis, covered in invisible sharp razor blades, filled with rage and anger, is jammed into your most delicate, life-giving birth canal. Hate-filled debris covers your sacred womb, the chalice of life defiled. Rage, hatred, and violence burrow into the walls of the uterus, wreaking inner havoc of dastardly proportions. Every nerve ending radiates how wrong you are; you are second-rate.

Your damaged soft tissues hold fear, shame, and self-hatred. Helplessness and hopelessness set in. The inner anguish continues to build—your ability to fend off masculine attacks evaporates. Your self-esteem plummets. The sexual abuse leaves you feeling like worthless scum. You're so busy despising yourself that there is little energy to flourish. The inner terror is overwhelming.

The Inner (R)Evolution:

• Approximately 70 women commit suicide every day in the US after being sexually abused.[6]

Sexual assault reverberates through the body, like an embedded computer chip, sending continuous signals that women are wrong, don't matter, and belong to the man. As a result, fear, trauma, and violence permeate society. Passed down in the lineage, taken for the way things are, 'normal' in the grown-up world. The global culture of women being inferior is in our corrupt DNA codes, neural programs and patterns, inherited beliefs, Matrices, Nasties, Bottom Sludge, and Veils of Illusion.

We all have masculine and feminine energies. So, every man has a woman inside; she is inferior, second-rate, and sexually abused. We must contemplate radical equality and its meaning in our bodies and lives. Until the 11th Childhood Circuitry transforms, we will continue perpetrating violence towards women.

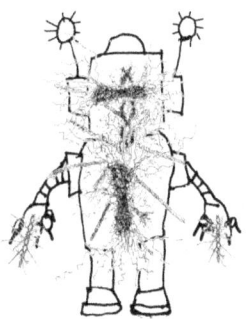

The inner feminine has trouble sorting out the Fear Bot from the inner masculine; the trauma is so entwined in the DNA. What she knows is the Fear Bot's version of patriarchy that poisons the 10th dimension.

Usurping feminine energy is the foundation for the current reality. Journey inside your trauma, corrupt DNA codes, and neural programming and discover the depths of the Fear Bots' manipulation.

As mentioned earlier, **women and girls put in 12.5 billion hours of unpaid care work every day — a contribution to the global economy of at least $10.8 trillion a year.**[7] Think about this for a minute and see where you fit into this shocking statistic. Take back your body and your power. Use your feminine energy to fuel and nurture your dreams, life, and body.

The 11th, squished down, constricted, contracted, and scared for eons, wants to expand. Healing and emerging take time. First, the wounded feminine must feel safe and accepted, and then she will reveal her secrets and power. The healed inner feminine is intuitive, magnetic, and sensual. She claims her self-worth and confidence. As she awakens, she radiates, igniting the 11th Soul Self to burst forth. A joyous, glorious opening into generous love and being. Freedom for the feminine to be seen, heard, and respected.

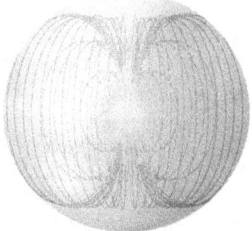

The feminine holds the keys to evolution and transformation. The way to evolve in each dimension is to follow your pleasure, what brings you joy, what makes you feel alive, and what makes you smile. Those feelings and sensations in your body are your guides. Your body knows the truth of who you are; it's not a mental concept; it's a deep inner knowing. The Soul Circuitry on the 11th holds your deep feminine wisdom.

Go beyond your linear, left brain, flow through your heart, all the way down to the divine feminine— into the cosmic flow of the universe. Call in your healed feminine wisdom, open to your magic and mystery —the pleasure of being you in your body. Ecstatic Secret Flow meanders into the nooks and crevices, winding through your body, breaking up all the blocks. Instead of conquering and overcoming fear, fear takes on a new flavor. To be deliciously eaten, devoured, savoring the gush of release, sensuous cascading flow. The deeper the release, the greater the pleasure.

You are the midwife to birth your worldview. Birth your voice, desires, and dreams. You are creating a new reality through the feminine. Call in your erotic, feminine energy.

Take up space and connect to your divine sacred essence to create a luscious, sensual embodiment—this is the path of evolution. A new merging, becoming one with the frequency of your feminine essence, flowing into cells, bathing neurons, flooding your body with your magical elixir. The river of life flows, iridescent translucent bubbles of joy dance on the Secret Flow, the blissful, sacred juice of life.

Your Soul Self aligns with specific feminine frequencies that want to be seen, come forward, and be a grander part of your life. And so, the question arises, who are you in the 11th dimension? What magic and mysteries want to be revealed? What are you here to birth?

The 12th Dimension - EMBODIMENT and FREEDOM

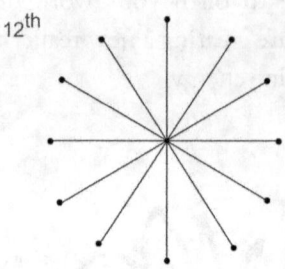

For weeks, soul fragments flutter into my Soul Circuitry, finding their unique docking stations to transport their joy and wisdom from far and near. What a joyous homecoming celebration.

A few days later, fluids spewed from every orifice in my body, puking my guts out for three days and nights. Streams of snot, waste baskets overflowing with used Kleenex. Retching, expelling the Bottom Sludge lies. Twisted realities erupt amongst bits of stinky, acidic vomit.

And then the next layer of blame ejects out my guts into the barf bowl by my bed. All the ways I blame men for creating me to be a victim. It's a layer of debris on top of my inner knowing. And this layer of the Bottom Sludge is the Fear Bot stealing my dreams, squishing my soul brilliance, all hiding the exciting, exhilarating, loving depths of who I am.

I'm cozy and warm, curled up in bed in a ball, hiding under the covers. I'm a safe little kid, yet, anger, fear, and blame loom. The stuck energy morphs into delicious delight. The Bottom Sludge slides, surging, careening out my body, releasing the path for clear, luminescent liquid light to wash and joyously bubble through my cells.

Layers of neural patterns and the matrix discharge. The programming around my organs that keeps them functioning in a specific way, shifts. Old skeletal system imprints release. It's like all the layers of the clear pages of an anatomy book have energies that kept me suppressed and in servitude to outside forces and resistant to change; now evacuate.

The Inner (R)Evolution:

No matter how wretched, despicable, or grotesque, that part is accepted and transformed with safety and love.

I sink further into the bedcovers. Here I am; I feel tiny and so excited to feel the safety I've never known in this lifetime.

A few days later, I slam up against an internal glass wall; all the illusions and distortions slide down the windowpane into a puddle of gooey muck, slimming around on the floor. I know I'm in the Fear Bots' control, but the struggle to move forward is unbearable. The oppression of victim consciousness is excruciating. I give thanks for how fucking hard it is. My self-compassion breaks up the solidified energies. At the same time, my Soul Circuitry rewires, connecting through the glass to the higher frequencies of my soul.

Close to my heart, in an unseen little silk purple bag with peachy pink lining and a gold cord holds the Trailblazer Technologies. The special tools to traverse the risky, perilous journey into freedom are always with me.

I'm seeing how I create the bad guys so I can play the victim role. A painful growing-up process of looking at my shit and observing the more profound ways I support the Fear Bot reality.

Later, moving all the aching, stuck places releases old, mysterious information. My belly starts to churn, and my feet tingle. Excitement mixed with fear rushes throughout my spine, igniting my body to full alert. The released energies and frequencies create images. Past lives flash before my eyes, making a streaming movie. The cartoon vision continues. Images flicker, layer upon layer of fucker/fuckee realities of illusion flash before my eyes. It's like watching an old-time movie; my neural circuitry, DNA. and the matrix create the inner play.

I'm in a birth canal, squishing victim consciousness out of my cells, bones, and thoughts. I continue dissolving into nothingness. The great void of the feminine tickled—my divine sacred erotic voluptuous juicy essence begins to flow. The pleasure of experiencing my soul essence with all of my senses is beyond momentary orgasmic delight. Full body enrapture, loving the soul source of who I am in every aspect of my being, bones, and ligaments.

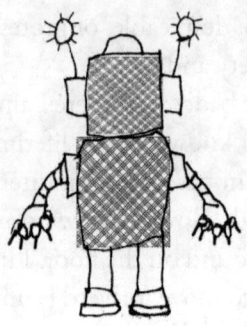

The 12th gets snarly—that's where there's a template scrambling your brain. In the 12th dimension, a matrix overlay mixes up the neural connections to keep fear dominant—a relic from the past, a component that we are outgrowing and evolving beyond. Developed way back in our lineage, it confines our thinking and behavior to fear and survival.

Unfortunately, it's not all light and sparkles; some of the most wicked deceptions live here. The 12th is concealed, holding the deepest secrets of the most profound darkness and the highest light. Hiding in the iridescent, luminous 12th, the Fear Bot is disgusting, corrupt, and vile. Deception and lies permeate the lower frequencies, perpetuating victim consciousness; the most refined discernment is necessary.

Instead of spreading fear, it's time for our brain function and neural programs to evolve beyond a seven-year-old, especially in the 12th dimension. The 12th has the neural system overlay of reptilian and victim consciousness that looks like a synthetic hologram, like a clear plastic coating that hides and seals in your brilliance and creates a shield to disconnect you from your soul essence and the cosmos.

Most DNA strands look similar, covered in shadows, toxic goo, suckers, and takers, suctioning off life force. However, sometimes the 12th DNA has an overlay that looks like a lizard. Underneath the creepy lizard skin is a layer of puffed-up white fluff, the arrogance of an inflated ego.

The Fear Bot's consciousness, a colossal beast, rules our bodies, supporting the current paradigm and patriarchy. A vast Nastie watches over, creating fear, pain, and disease by stealing life-giving, nurturing energy.

The Inner (R)Evolution:

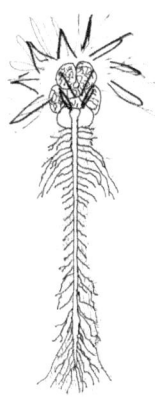

Perched on top of the spine in the 12th dimension, the Nastie dupes humanity into believing he is God. His goal is to keep people divided, fighting against each other—religion, politics, and the masculine and feminine energies in the body. The Fear Bot consciousness, a chameleon trying to blend in, clings for life; this is where significant mind manipulation occurs.

The lizard's head is in the 12th, and the reptilian body and tail spiral down the spine, through the dimensions, around the coccyx. The Fear Bot's neural programs strangle the spinal column. Tiny neuron tentacles dig into the spinal fluid, stealing nourishment to feed fear-based brain parts. The death grip, sharp fangs, and spiky claws keep you barely alive to suck off your life-giving feminine energy; this viral Fear Bot infects humanity.

A good example is COVID. The Fear Bot consciousness supports COVID, a low-frequency unnatural virus that triggers massive fear of death. To me, the vaccines look like neon blue razor-sharp computer chips designed to cut through tissues, nerves, and cellular structures, thus compromising the immune system.

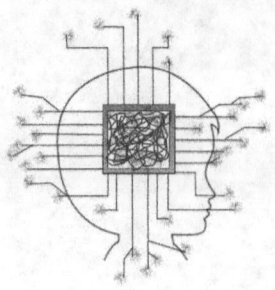

Our Childhood Circuitry feeds on fear, suffering, and struggle; we are wired to carry the frequency of victimhood. Blinders keep us from seeing our victimhood. It's much easier to notice others than to perceive victim consciousness in ourselves. We want to blame them, fix them, and change them to fit our mold of how we think they are supposed to be. We are angry and afraid to see the truth of who we are. It's much easier to blame our boss, partners, friends, the government, or the system than to look inside. Everyone else is to blame; therefore, we don't have to take responsibility for our inner suffering, trauma, and victimhood.

The seeds of victim consciousness live in the 12th. Low-level frequencies form a cover of suffering, sacrifice, and scapegoat consciousness designed to keep you small, unseen, and unheard. The blanket is so dense, massive, and heavy you feel exhausted, and it's hard to discover what's happening. When scrunched up under the oppressive, suffocating blankets of victim consciousness, it's hard to stand up, take a deep breath, and believe in yourself. It feels like the only way to survive is to keep eating victim sludge.

The victim pattern is addictive, worse than sugar, alcohol, or cigarettes. To grow up beyond seven-year-olds, we must take responsibility and quit playing the victim card. The only way to end the madness is to stop engaging in the game. Victim consciousness keeps the cycle going.

The Inner (R)Evolution:

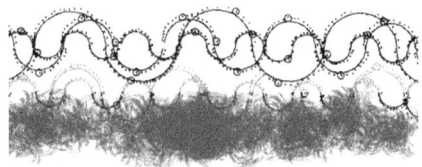

Bring Secret Flow to your victim consciousness; the high frequencies break up and dissolve the oppressive mantle of martyr frequencies. Notice how your body feels as the Secret Flow loosens and releases the grip that shuts down your energy and keeps you immobilized and stuck. Freedom is transforming the conscious and unconscious programs that run your life, moving from victim consciousness to the sovereignty to be all of you.

The Fear Bot's vast, far-reaching power and control on the 12th is profound. Great courage and tenacity are required. It's imperative to distinguish the artificial and victim consciousness from your soul source energy. Evolve from fear to higher mental functions, from pretzel thinking to clarity.

Discover how to discern between organic and non-organic consciousness. Are you listening to your soul or the counterfeit holographic inserts from outside influences? The insight gets more refined. Keep asking yourself, is this the Fear Bot or my Soul Self? To disconnect victim consciousness wiring, change your wiring to the blueprint of your soul, your Soul Circuitry.

This isn't some fairytale; this is your life. What do you choose? You can rewire your neurology to connect to your Soul Circuitry; use Secret Flow to assist in releasing the crafty, cunning Fear Bot and victim consciousness.

Maintain your inner freedom by shifting your neural programming from anger, rage, and victimhood and connecting to the truth of who you are. The domain of sovereignty, inner liberty, and power, it's not a process of denying your inner feelings and fears. The journey HOME, transforming the beliefs and stories you believed about who you are, and having the clarity to look beyond the lies and see who you are. Have deep compassion, forgiveness, and gratitude for yourself. You are a part of creating a new humanity and reality. A profound feat to accomplish occurs minute by minute throughout your day and life.

Claim your power; your life-giving juice gives birth to the new. Welcome every part of you, all the different aspects and frequencies of who you are. All beautifully housed in your Soul Circuitry, there is a special place for you in every dimension that holds your genius and uniqueness. The you you've always dreamed about, here, safe, and ready to play.

The 12 dimensions together create a picture of the reality that only you inhabit. Whatever happens in each dimension filters how you see and live in the world. As you clean out the blind spots, a vast range of possibilities opens up.

We've just explored how the Fear Bot works on the first 12 dimensions, and it might have stirred up some stuff as you read. It's OK; we are all run by the Fear Bot. Until we clean them out, the bot has a hold. Imagine inheriting a huge house filled with junk—floor to ceiling. There's a tiny path to navigate and function marginally.

You would think it would be easy to clean out the house, but it's terrifying. You don't know what is lurking behind the hidden doors. Would Nasties have taken up residence and fed on the inner debris? What slurs and creeps in the basement?

But, as you clean out the house, you discover hidden treasures. So keep cleaning, and you'll uncover the home of your dreams with space for all of who you are to play, create and have fun with others. Creating a new reality comes from play and pleasure.

Come home to you. Joyous pleasure and freedom to be who you are on as many dimensions as you like. This book is about the first 12, but many more dimensions exist. Keep asking, where are my blind spots? What am I not seeing? You're not asking some outside authority; you are talking with yourself, your body, and your cells.

Soul Self

For five decades, in the 12th dimension, the Council of Twelve surrounded my body whenever Shakti was in her full force. The Council of Twelve was a group of spiritual beings, Ascended Masters, that watched over me.

It took me years to realize that the Ascended Masters connect with the Fear Bot and the Childhood Circuitry. Ascended Masters shrouded in artificial white light, out the top of the head, linked to a hierarchy, disconnected from the feminine—the lopsided version of evolution. Great beings in the sky, dedicated to the Fear Bot, show us how to continue the distorted reality illusion.

Your own Council of Twelve evolves; your 12 dimensions surround you, not someone else's, not some saint who stole your energy. The joining of all your multidimensional Soul Selves takes place on the 12th.

Cut off during trauma, denied connections for lifetimes, and long-lost information, your soul fragments arrive with protection. Your missing components, floating around in space, hiding in the ethers, return home. Your most profound aspects are finally welcomed, honored, and cherished. The deep safety, home, being embodied.

How would it feel for your Soul Self in every dimension to unconditionally love each other? Lovers, dancing in joy, exuding delight; all your superpowers—angel wings, magic wands, sparkles, voluptuous power, tantalizing pleasure. The pleasure of embodying your Soul Self is profound. Your purpose, passion, and enjoyment are expressed and lived fully. Call together your superpowers on all dimensions. The innate intelligence of your body knows the way.

Celebrate each time an aspect of a dimension grounds into your Soul Circuitry. Enjoy the incredible evolution and awakening process by rooting your energies into the earth. Every cell, nerve, and bone connects to your multidimensional wisdom and inner knowing.

Your Soul Self is the person you've always wanted to be. The one you look up to and dream about becoming, the inner fulfillment and connection you crave. The Soul Self encompasses all of who you are.

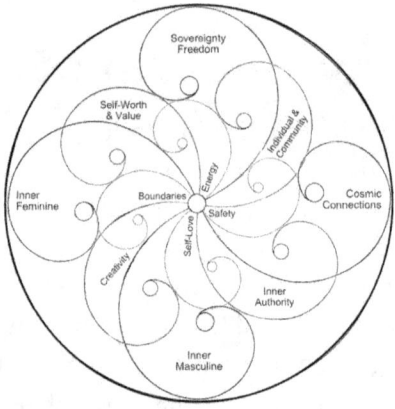

The 12th Soul Self is the vehicle for the breathtaking dive into uncertainty, a joyous adventure we've been preparing for lifetimes—the delicious descent into pleasure and love for the highest good of all. Soul food and divine essence fill every starving nook and cranny in your body, every cell nourished.

The embodied Soul Self is the composite of all your magnificent aspects. The ray of your light penetrates and merges with the earth, changing the frequency of the world and the cosmos. You are the transmitter and receiver, the grounding rod, the vehicle of awakening and uniting cosmic frequencies into the earth.

Your Soul Self brings the cosmos's magic, wisdom, and mysteries to physical reality, information from twelve dimensions (and more) to earth to help create a new you and reality. Innocent gratitude permeates your reality; you feel alive, pulsating with joy.

PART III

CLAIM YOUR MULTIDIMENSIONAL SOUL SELF

Discover the magic and mystery of navigating and empowering your body. You're learning to become a coder, a programmer, the technician of your life. You're discovering how to rewire your nervous system, reconfigure your DNA, and dissolve matrices with the Trailblazer Technologies. Instead of unseen forces being in charge, you can take control of your body—an astounding accomplishment. Claim your Soul Self, the essence of who you are on each dimension, also known as your authentic self or higher self.

This model makes it easier to step out of the muck and see a clear path to escape the inner morass where your brain turns to mush and you're falling fast into the pit of despair.

I used to feel like unlovable scum, filled with inner torment, self-hatred, and unworthiness. When I used the term unlovable scum, people scoffed. They had no concept of what was hiding inside. I was a master at putting up a façade, wearing a mask that everything was OK. I was terrified for anyone to see the depth of horror inside my body.

Since I started using the Trailblazer Technologies daily, I no longer have crippling panic attacks; my PTSD has almost dissolved. My decades of waking up in the night screaming with horrific nightmares no longer happen. The electroshock that zapped the back of my neck for over sixty-five years is gone. My trigeminal neuralgia, the supposedly incurable disease that feels like an infected tooth, a sinus headache, and a migraine all at the same time, no longer triggers searing, devastating pain and suicidal thoughts.

And now, the feelings of worthlessness and inner horror are gone. Instead, I feel whole, complete, and loved. Daily I love and appreciate myself more.

No more inner critic screams how wretched I am; inner peace expands. The depth of freedom to be me is profound. A pure innocence arises; I feel clean inside. From the space of clarity, my life takes on a new meaning.

I'm not implying that this model will necessarily heal your body; that's up to you and your soul essence. But I know taking control of your body leads to profound love, gratitude, and acceptance of who you choose to be in this lifetime.

I challenge you to do the work to discover who you really are, your values, and what you choose to create—a far-reaching map. A leap of consciousness is required to visualize something never created or imagined before.

In the following chapters, we will discover the necessary preparations and the step-by-step process to dissolve the Fear Bot, shift your neurology and DNA, and reclaim your life.

9. PREPARATIONS

Before we explore transforming the Fear Bot and using the Trailblazer Technologies, it's important to prepare. Read on and discover how to create a safe space, set your intention, and find ways to connect with your body's innate wisdom. We will also explore the importance of grounding and connecting to the earth.

Safety and Cocooning

Sometimes you don't feel safe; there's nowhere to hide because what's happening inside is different from what's happening outside. So you live in two realities, the inner and the outer, one unconscious and the other conscious.

Without inner safety, you feel hopeless, vulnerable, a helpless victim. Nothing can happen without protection. For your body and nervous system to change, security is required. If your nervous system is triggered, it will revert to its old programmed path. Your body needs to feel safe, vulnerable, open, held in love, accepted just as you are, and in non-judgmental love.

Tip:

Wear a hoodie, protecting your spine, neck, and brain, creating safety in your nervous system.

Create a safe, sacred space in your home to journal, explore, and go within.

When your body is transforming or feels unsafe, turn off your TV, computer, and phone. Get in a quiet space and close the door. Lay on your bed or a comfy couch with your spine protected by pillows. Curl

The Inner (R)Evolution:

up under a blanket, and take a few deep breaths. Protect your spine so your body feels physically secure for the innate healing mechanisms to create profound inner transformation. Surround your body with Spirals of Love and Gratitude and Light Codes. Create your safe nest, your cocoon of transformation. Now do the process outlined in Chapter 8.

The people around you may not want you to change; it's a scary process that triggers their inner fears. And, when you start being more you, your energy permits others to dive in deeper to discover who they are. But, no matter what your partners, relatives, or friends say, empower yourself to be you; they will adapt eventually or not. Feeling safe brings an intense depth of inner freedom to be yourself that far outweighs the opposition.

Living in fear is exhausting; living with inner safety is refreshing. The Inner (R)Evolution is a journey of being held in security; your Soul Circuitry, your essence, and source have your back; it's safe to be you. You're secure—all of your weird, strange, eccentric parts.

INTENTION AND PERMISSION

Your intention sets the trajectory of your journey and is a tool for manifestation. Who do you want to evolve into now? What do you want to birth, to bring into form on earth?

Your intention broadcasts all the time. But are the signals coming from your unconscious or your conscious desires? Do your hidden beliefs support or sabotage your intentions? Changing focus is an easy concept, yet so tricky when neural programs cemented in, like heavy metal beams and rusted rebar, the framework of your life holds your ancestors' behaviors, thoughts, and beliefs.

Imagine you are shooting an arrow into the vast cosmos of infinite potential. The more focused and pinpointed, the better. State precisely what you want, don't be vague or wishy-washy.

Your intention is a laser beam focus in alignment with your soul frequency rather than the collective unconscious, directing your energy to a specific realm in the vast, open field of possibility. When aligned with who you are, your goal rides on the frequency of your soul, traveling the cosmos, picking up resources, and connecting events and people to bring your heartfelt, passion-filled desires to you on earth.

Our brains can't distinguish between a thought and an action. So, visualize your intention, feel it, and believe it. Imagine you are living your dreams now. The more fuel, the farther it will reach, returning with magic, miracles, and enjoyment. Joy and pleasure are the juicy energies to rocket your intention. Like cosmic honey, delight attracts the luscious, loving frequencies, people, and dynamism needed to birth your desires.

Coherent waveforms travel great distances; incoherent waveforms dissipate quickly. The more aligned with your soul's frequency, the further the wave reaches.

Each person's compass will point in a distinct direction because we each have something particular to contribute. The compass is your values, dreams, and focus. If this comes from a place of pushing, forcing, and struggle, you're following an off-track external commitment. But, if what you are doing brings you joy and pleasure, lights up your life, and is for the highest good of all, you are on target.

You are manifesting a new reality based on your dreams. Establish your world, your daily life, so you're living your vision, but it's grounded, thriving, and lusciously abundant here on earth. Deliciously satisfying. Savor the comfort of safety, knowing you are worthy, protected, and everything aligns with your soul essence.

It's two-way communication, sending out your intention and receiv-

The Inner (R)Evolution:

ing. Give yourself permission to receive. If unworthiness crops up, surround it with Spirals of Love and Gratitude and watch it dissolve. Open to receive miraculous abundance, joy, and your heart's desires.

Also, permit yourself to take the next steps. Your body needs to know it's OK to let go of the old it's been carrying for decades, lifetimes, eons.

TIP:

State your intentions out loud; your voice informs your cells and body. For example, say out loud: "I give my body permission to evolve into the next version of me."

Reality is spiraling into form; evolve into who you came here to be.

INNER KNOWING AND MUSCLE TESTING

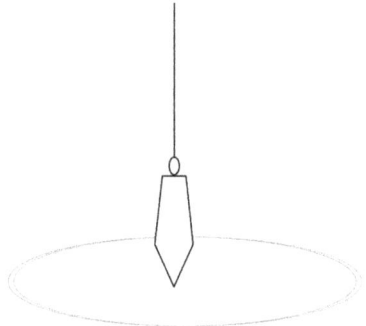

The tricky part, of course, is what or who to trust. What is true? How do you know for sure? Hiding under all the layers of what you're told to do, your body knows the truth for you. As you embark on this journey, you will want to have a way to check in with your body's innate wisdom to discover what is happening in each dimension.

Explore different ways of muscle testing, using a pendulum, and connecting to your inner knowing. There are many quick and effective muscle testing techniques. Discover which is the most reliable for you.

You will use this to determine what dimension is activated and which of the Fear Bot's blocks needs attention. It's fun to detect where it is hiding and which Trailblazer Technologies to use to assist in your wondrous evolution.

A way to communicate with your body and unconscious; self-muscle testing reveals fantastic information. It's essential to clarify what you are asking and be specific. Your response can only be as clear as the clarity of the question. You may want to ask the question in various ways to get an accurate answer.

One of my favorite ways to do muscle tests is the whole-body sway test. First, stand in a relaxed and comfortable position. Keep your knees loose and slightly bent. To begin, ask obvious yes/no questions, for example:

My name is (say your name)
My name is (say someone else's name)
I live in (say where you live)
I live in (say someplace you don't live)

When it's a yes or positive response, your body moves forward. Your body moves backward when it's a negative response.

Then, start testing to see what dimension needs attention.

Say you notice a deep heartbreak feeling. Ask: "Is this deep aching pain in my heart in the first dimension?" The answer comes up no.

"Is this deep aching pain in my heart in the second dimension?"

Let's imagine you discover it's in the 10th dimension. The 10th is related to patriarchy and unhealed or disempowered masculinity. So perhaps your next question is, "Is this pain in my heart related to my father?" Yes, the muscle testing reveals.

And continue:

"Is this deep pain in my heart lurking in the Bottom Sludge?"

Go through the Fear Bot list, and see what the muscle testing reveals.

"Is this pain from my ancestry passed down in my neural programs?"

"Is this pain mine?"

"Is this my deeper truth?"

"Is this the Fear Bot?"

The Inner (R)Evolution:

Another way would be to say, "My name is Fear Bot."

Then say, my name is (say your name), and watch to see how your body responds.

Follow the sensations in your body. If the pain is increasing, you're onto something. There might be a Nastie trying to scare you away, telling you this won't work.

Then resistance might kick in; the dishes need washing; maybe I should check my email. Then, with firmness and conviction, bring in the spirals of gratitude and thank the Nasties, resistance, and whatever comes up. Use all of the Trailblazer Technologies and see which ones work best.

Chapter 8 describes all the steps in the process. For now, it is essential to discover how to tune into your deepest authentic self. Over time you will develop your methods of inner discernment. If you like, you can check online to find other muscle-testing techniques. For example, some people enjoy using a pendulum.

You are discovering how to reparent your childhood neural programs and release the Fear Bot from your body, mind, and energy field on multiple dimensions. Muscle testing brings clarity from the body's innate intelligence rather than the pre-programmed bias.

As you work with the dimensions, your inner knowing will sharpen. You will learn to trust your guts and intuition as you connect more deeply to the essence of who you are. And then, it's important to connect with the earth.

. . .

DR. CYNTHIA MILLER

Grounding

Back in the 1970s, for five years, I rowed boats and slept on the banks of the river. I felt so held, loved, and supported. It was one of the happiest, most magical times of my life.

OVER THE YEARS, THE SAFETY IN MY NERVOUS SYSTEM diminished. Bombarded daily with city life, electronics, rubber shoes, living indoors, and being insulated from nature that I love so deeply. As a result, I kept getting sicker, felt crappy, and more depressed. For years, I couldn't pinpoint what I longed for and missed. Finally, I discovered that grounding restored my vitality—the connection to mother earth provided profound safety to my nervous system so I could transform.

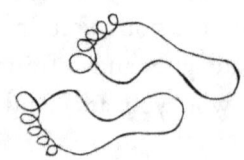

Three things happen as we leave the lofty confines of the head and connect our feet to the earth.
1. We release toxins into the earth
2. We receive earth's nurturing energy
3. We connect to multidimensional information and awaken

1. WE RELEASE TOXINS INTO THE EARTH

If you aren't grounded, the toxins build. No amount of healthy organic food, yoga, and meditation will remove the Fear Bot's toxic frequencies from your body. Internal pollution builds up, creating disease, depression, and sickness. An energetic connection occurs when you put your bare feet on the earth. Ask the ground for permission to release the toxins and feel the energies naturally flow out of your feet.

Sometimes resistance comes up about connecting to our dear mother, the giver of life, the source of all nourishment in the 3rd dimension. Yet, without our connection to the earth, we die.

TIP:
Walk barefoot on the earth, sit under a tree, and play outside.

2. WE RECEIVE EARTH'S NURTURING ENERGY

For healing to occur, our nervous system and cellular structures need to change and transform. Cellular transformation can only happen when the body and nervous system feel safe enough to let go of the old. Safety is in direct relationship to our connection to mother earth. Without that connection, the body doesn't feel safe enough for a profound transformation.

When we are in our heads, disconnected from our feminine essence, detached from our feet, we get off-kilter. The current reality and chaos we live in are related to our separation from the earth, which nurtures and supports all life.

When your energy is grounded in the earth, it doesn't get stolen.

Safely connected and hidden in the depths of mother Gaia, the Fear Bot can't discover and usurp your energy.

TIP:
You can buy mattress pads and other tools to ground you throughout the day and night.

3. **CONNECT MULTIDIMENSIONAL INFORMATION**, AND create space in our bodies for our multifaceted brilliance.

As the toxins leave your body, streams of multidimensional cosmic energies have a place to land and connect to the earth. You are a receptor for the highest cosmic frequencies, powers, and technologies that will assist your evolution. Open into the vast multidimensional being that you are. But that can't happen unless you connect to the earth. If ungrounded, your magical gifts have nowhere to land and form in the 3rd dimension.

It's time to unite the earth's wisdom and the universe's magic. You are a connecting rod, a vehicle for creating a new reality, new humanity, and a bridge between the earth and the cosmos. You are here to contribute your unique perspective and brilliance to this magical, mysterious unfolding. With your embodiment comes profound wisdom.

TIP:
As you walk barefoot or sit on the ground, invite your cosmic energies to connect to the earth. Notice how it feels to root your galactic wisdom into your body and the land.

One beautiful way is to walk barefoot on the earth. This is because your soul and the sole of your feet connect to the earth.

The journey is not about ascension, leaving your body, or going out the top of your head in meditation. It's about embodiment, coming fully into your body. So chase out all the toxic trash, the inner critic, feeling worthless. Kick them all out. They are not the truth of who you are.

New seeing emerges, and fresh synapses trigger, creating further neural pathways connecting divergent areas of your brain. As a result, narrow-minded thinking dissolves as you join the cosmic energies to the earth.

Ground into the earth and feel the pain in your body ease as the toxins are released. Experience the loving, nurturing energy of the planet. Connect your cosmic brilliance with the earth to manifest your magical reality and become the person you came to earth to be.

10. THE PROCESS

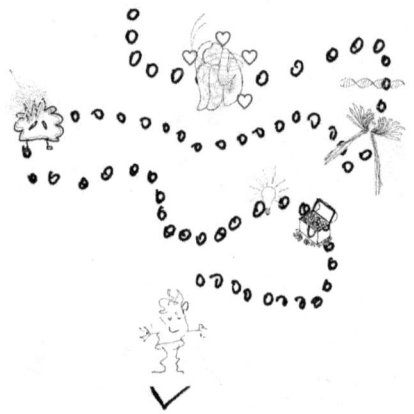

THE INNER (R)EVOLUTION IS AN INVITATION TO GREATER self-empowerment. Establish your daily twenty-minute check-ins, observe what's happening inside, use the tools, and watch your life transform. A fulfilling daily practice, drip by drip, leads to astonishing results—not a meditation practice where the goal is to still the mind, or Nirvana, where your mind and body are disconnected and ungrounded. But a grand adventure of claiming your body and freedom.

There is nothing to fix, rip out, or cut out; you aren't broken. You are not the problem. Your body tells you something is wrong; instead of blaming yourself, it's the corrupt system, the Fear Bot. In the old wiring,

The Inner (R)Evolution:

your life-giving energy it's siphoned off and used to support and finance the wealth of a few.

Learning how to use each tool, discovering how to go inside, and finding where things are on each dimension takes time; it's a practice. It's not an overnight fix. It's not a 30-day guarantee program. Instead, an internal shift; how do you choose to live your life? What do you value? How do you want to experience your body?

The key is to use the tools daily, sometimes moment to moment; that's where the transformation happens. Commitment and consistency are fundamental. The layers and nuances of self-hatred, abandonment, and unworthiness are astonishing; more and more keep arising to clear.

Start a daily practice of exploring the feelings in your body with curiosity rather than dread, overwhelm, and worry. The path evolves into pleasure—the prohibited realm of the feminine. The forbidden territory of enjoyment is cut off, denied, and made wrong by the Fear Bot reality.

Keep following pleasure. But, sometimes, an inner revolution occurs; the old is disrupted and wants to regain control. Inner riots will break out if you abandon the pain to feel joy. Your body is programmed to follow the neural circuit sequences to create a fucker/fuckee world.

We're creating a new sustainable, self-discovery, curiosity adventure. Give yourself permission to deepen your self-exploration. A jigsaw puzzle, rearranging the pieces, creates a new image, reality, and life. Woven together with multiple layers of who you are.

You may have a specific issue that you're working on, feel confused, or know something is off, but you don't know what. So when triggered by life, do the process—a daily commitment to discovering your next step.

Rewiring takes place in stages and jumps from one dimension to another according to your body's innate intelligence. It's not a direct path; it meanders, twists, and turns. Always different, discovering hidden crevices that are ready to reveal inner truths.

PART I The Process

1. Set up your space
   a. Create a safe cocoon for your transformation, on the couch, or in bed, with pillows supporting your spine. Spiral Love and Gratitude all around the room you are in and your body.
   b. Set your intention.
   c. Invite your body to merge with your Soul Circuitry.

2. Muscle Testing
   a. Use muscle testing to see what dimension is activated. Knowing the dimension will give you clues about what's happening, and you will be able to transmute the energy more efficiently.
   b. Muscle test to discern which part of the Fear Bot is activated, if it's in the Bottom Sludge, neural programs, corrupt DNA codes, Nasties, etc.
   c. Go through the list of Trailblazer Technologies and see which ones will assist.

3. You may hit resistance.
   a. Your mind may tell you that this won't work for you. Your body may scream in discomfort.
   b. Keep going; use different Trailblazer Technologies to clean out the resistance and old junk.

. . .

4. Your body relaxes; the old energies and frequencies start to ooze out of your body.
   a. Keep going until there is a breakthrough, which may take time.
   b. Dive in deeper until the inner angst morphs into joy and pleasure.

5. Give your body, neural programs, and DNA permission to evolve.
   a. Your body has received messages from the Fear Bot for your whole life.
   b. Keep giving your cells, nerves, and bones permission to evolve, permission to listen to the language of your soul rather than the inner critic and Fear Bot.
   c. To become free, you must give the energies inside you their freedom, and then you will become free.
   d. Keep going. You can do this.

6. Unplug your energy from the Fear Bot.
   a. Invite your soul frequency to fill all the places where the Fear Bot resided in your body.
   b. Plug your energy into your Soul Circuitry.
   c. Invite your nervous system to relax and rewire to the new higher frequencies in your body.
   d. Timelines collapse, past, present, and future merge. Your co-creative powers expand.

7. Once the Soul Circuitry and soul frequency are in place, there is space and an area for your Soul Self to land and flourish.

8. Give thanks for the profound transformation that is occurring.
   a. Thank your body for all it has experienced. Ask what she/he needs.

b. You are the only one that knows the exact frequency that your body needs. Send that frequency to your body; like a homeopathic, your body shifts.

9. **You'll know you're complete when your body feels** joyous inside.

For handy reference, download the checklists at DrCynthiaMiller.com/checklists.

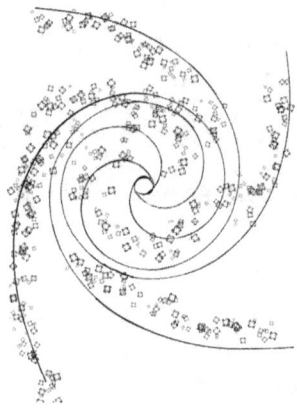

GIVE YOURSELF PERMISSION TO CREATE A PROCESS THAT IS most natural for you, but be sure to include all the steps in what order works for your body. You may go back and forth with the above steps. Sometimes it takes time for all the puzzle pieces to fall into place so that the neurology shifts in the cellular structures on multiple dimensions. When everything lines up, then your soul essence flows through your body.

Sometimes when I've had an extensive clearing, a cascade of fear and doubt fill the vacant space. Kick them out and fill your space with you, your soul frequency, the juice of your life.

You may work on one thing for weeks; **you are rewiring thou-**

sands of years of old corrupt patterns and DNA. Follow the flow, a meandering, looping, spiraling journey through your body, transforming fears and expanding into delight. Joy will bubble up from your depths.

You will jump from dimension to dimension; it's not a linear process. For example, you may clear the Bottom Sludge on the 5th, your neural programs on the 10th, the matrix on the 6th, and then your Soul Self on the 8th is ready to expand—a journey through a magical landscape, where each step reveals in perfect timing. Be gentle with yourself. It takes time to clear out layers of junk, clean up your DNA, and disconnect from the Fear Bot.

Keep digging. It's all inside you, hidden by the Fear Bot to keep you in servitude. It's an inner job. So keep unplugging, rewiring, and out of the grasp of the Fear Bot into your Soul Circuitry, the essence of you. Not an imposed system designed to suck you dry and make you feel inadequate and small.

How do you know the truth for you? That's when you use kinesiology or a pendulum to help discover your soul's guidance from the screaming, fearful, nagging voice of the Fear Bot.

It's in your body; your neurology is yours. You have the power and the Trailblazer Technologies to forge your soul's path. The path of surrendering into your feminine. The further you go, the more exciting it gets. The colossal fear blocks keep melting; smaller things appear to be cleaned and cleared. Going deeper, tiny seeds that created the entire entangled Childhood Circuitry untangle.

Inner peace and contentment radiate. Expand into the iridescent, luminescent rays of all that is, oneness, love, and soul connection. We are all connected to existence. Sinking. Swirling, spiraling DNA, traveling the vast cosmos. Let go of the suffering and follow the pleasure. The path is down and in, into the depths of your body and soul.

PART II SELF-CARE, INTEGRATION, AND PLAYTIME
To further your integration, use the ideas below.

1. IT IS VITAL TO GROUND YOUR NEW ENERGIES. FOR example, sit on the grass, and put your back against a tree. Or use a grounding mattress pad. You are bringing new parts of your soul essence and multidimensions to earth.

2. DRINK LOTS OF WATER. YOU'VE RELEASED A LOT OF OLD stuff, and drinking water will help to clear it out of your body.

3. NAPS AND COCOONING; REST WHEN YOU NEED TO. When your body is rewiring, it requires a lot of energy. Sometimes you only need 10 or 15 minutes for the process to happen. When this occurs, ensure your spine is protected; in bed, under the covers is best.

4. DITHERING - WANDERING AROUND AIMLESSLY. NOT SURE where you are going or what you're supposed to do. Your mind may start beating you up, telling you to get on track and be productive; after all, you have bills to pay and things to do. But, dithering is an essential

part of the integration process. Your body is integrating the new while the old is leaving, which leaves a gap; the old known way is no longer in place, and the new isn't established yet. So, invite the dithering to play and have fun. Whatever feels good at the moment. Notice what happens.

5. SCRIBBLING, DOODLING, COLORING – LET IT ALL OUT, AND write in your journal with no editing.

6. MOVEMENT - AN INNER DANCE ERUPTS FROM YOUR SOUL, where your body jerks and spasms. Your body moves in strange foreign ways. Unusual weird sounds expel from your guts. Instead of resisting, get curious, dive in deeper, follow what feels good, and explore. Breathe into these areas, and move to expand into your inner feminine—the keeper of inner wisdom, alchemy, and delight.

7. INVITE YOUR SOUL FREQUENCY TO GLIDE DEEP WITHIN your body, lubricating the network of your life with juicy love and play. Exquisite new connections, flowing crystals, sliding between a flowing liquid and a crystalline structure. A slippery slope into the land of the forbidden feminine. This level of inner nourishment is prohibited in the old reality.

It's your body, soul, frequency, and life-giving energy. So you have full permission to use your energy however you like.

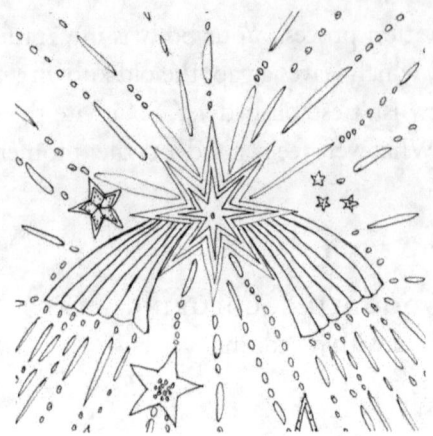

PART III Your Vision

How is your vision for your future evolving? How does it feel? You are creating a new worldview. What do you choose to add today? Write your thoughts, feelings, and ideas in your journal.

What is one action step you can take today? Take one easy action step a day that can be incorporated into your life, leading to massive change. However, if you try to add too many new things at once, you may feel overwhelmed, and nothing will last.

Perhaps it's changing how you use the rooms in your house to have more places to play and have fun. Or discover a new way of self-care so your body feels more loved. You are creating a new life that supports your joy and awakening. Follow your spontaneity, and do something out of the ordinary that makes you happy.

Keep playing with the Trailblazing Technologies.

You may find one tool that works best on specific aspects of the Fear Bot. Some tools may resonate more deeply than others; that's perfect. As you dive deeper and discover your magic on different dimensions, bring these technologies to your life and work. Over time you will find how profound these technologies are.

Play with the Trailblazer Technologies until you are very familiar with how each one works and how they work together. Then, bring in your magic; add your wisdom and brilliance to your life toolkit.

Keep building your Trailblazer Technologies toolkit, a first aid kit to move from victim consciousness, constriction, and fear into joyous, radiant freedom. I'm sure you already have tools to assist your awakening, which may include wonderful things like breath work, bodywork, gem elixirs, flower essences, etc. Incorporate the 12 dimensions of you and discover your style of wizardry in alignment with your core values, wondrous gifts, and pleasure.

This is a lifelong process as you awaken into a richer life, inner fulfillment, more profound joy, and lightness while creating a new reality beyond the worldview of your ancestors, forging the path into a brave new humanity. Have fun and enjoy the journey of self-discovery and freedom.

Over time, a new you emerges—evolving into more extraordinary aspects of your magnificent self.

11. EXPLORING DEEPER

Here are some guideposts you may encounter to assist your unique exploration into the wild unknown of being free of the Fear Bot.

The Great Divide
Have you noticed the energies are changing? The great divide is becoming more visible, a parting of the seeing.

The Inner (R)Evolution:

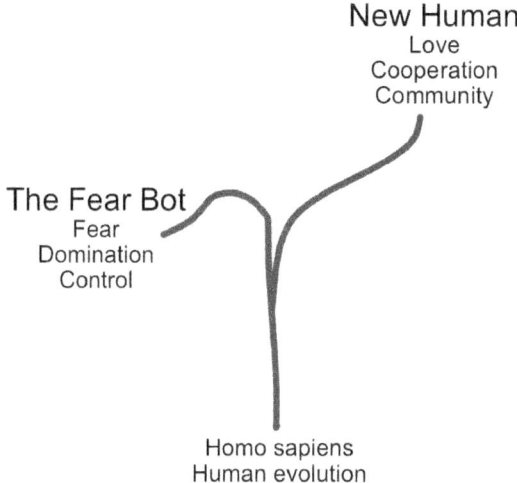

The old paradigm of fear, manipulation, domination, and control is on one side. Yet, another reality exists on love, connection, and generosity. To go from one reality to the other is like stepping through a portal.

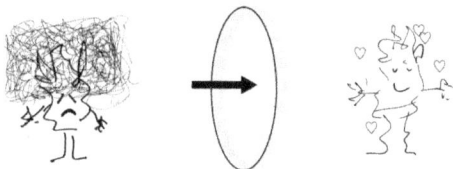

The journey through the portal requires leaving behind your old baggage. You must rewire your body. The low-frequency fear can't exist in the high frequency of the new reality. Instead, you need to upgrade to access your brilliance, deep joy, and playful, loving essence. As you release the old, you connect to the core of who you are on multiple dimensions, and a new self emerges.

The world is in chaos and flux. So it's the perfect time to go for it; cook up what you want. Take one step a day. Watch an exciting path open up, not knowing what will unfold in the next hour, week, or month.

Karmic Glue

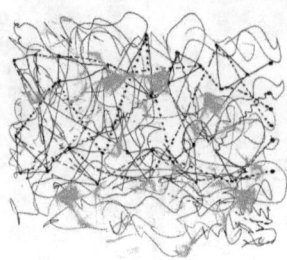

I met a man online, and as we spoke on a video call, sparks flew, heart-opening, a rush of tremendous connection. His response was this was the energy of soul mates or twin flames. I had a different reaction. I remembered similar energy exchanges at the beginning of past intense relationships. I used muscle testing and discovered we'd been together in thirty past lives exchanging roles of father, mother, son, daughter, brother, sister, friend, lover, perpetrator, victim, and enemy.

Together we cleared the past betrayal, hurt, manipulation, sexual abusers and abused, and patterns of superiority/inferiority. It takes incredible courage to see our hidden, dastardly deeds. The clearing produced lightness, inner freedom, and clarity.

Traversing dimensions and timelines and clearing out old junk, you may encounter Karmic Glue. Karma is related to the cycle of cause and effect. According to this theory, what happens to a person results from their actions. Good deeds create positive Karma, while bad deeds create negative Karma, misfortune, and suffering. Karmic Glue attracts and traps low-frequency energies, emotions, and neural patterns like sticky molasses or gooey tar. Imagine being entangled and entwined with jealousy or having green threads of envy tightly woven around your body. The Karmic Glue holds this rat's nest of low frequencies in place, which triggers old patterns in our current lives.

A karmic thread passes through lifetimes, influencing today's events, feelings, and thoughts. The sticky glue increases with each lifetime. Karmic attachments run deep; envy, shame, and abandonment consume many connections —the stuff of soap operas, jealousy, betrayal, and infidelity. Current lifetime relationships become murky; interactions trigger

The Inner (R)Evolution:

ancient karmic patterns. Some of our more difficult relationships carry a lot of toxic karmic sludge.

The veils of forgetfulness reconstruct and appear with each new lifetime; it's like starting from the beginning. So, I encourage you to explore the possibility of past lives and clear the Karmic Glue. It may save you years of grief, heartbreak, and trauma.

Each lifetime explores what it is to be a human being. We've played all the roles, victim, perpetrator, good girl, bad guy, heroine, and villain.

The low-level energies, emotions, and behaviors will keep reappearing until they transform to a higher frequency. The process of conscious evolution invites you to explore your unconscious hatred, jealousies, and sabotaging patterns and bring them up to consciousness. The karmic patterns keep repeating, playing out, creating the current reality of fear, violence, and drama.

As we evolve, the illusions drop, and we see more of the depth of who we are. The Trailblazer Technologies of Spirals of Gratitude, Light Codes, and Secret Flow work well to release the Karmic Glue. Removing the Bottom Sludge reveals your dazzling brilliance.

To become free, you must give the others inside you and your past lives their freedom. And then you will become free. The joy of releasing past lives is delightful. The captive energy is released, untwisting pain and suffering into pleasure, and your brilliance magnifies.

RECEIVERS AND DECODERS

We are awakening to frequencies beyond the 3-D bandwidth. Each dimension has a unique set of receivers that decode the messages.

Low-frequency receivers continually broadcast fear into your body. An external equivalent is a TV, a continuous blast of news created by the Fear Bot, filled with fury, tragedy, and suffering, designed to keep your nervous system on high alert. As a result, your brilliant thoughts receive no juice; all your life force is devoted to survival. No matter how much money you have or what precautions you've taken, life and the future is filled with apprehension. The Fear Bot wants you to live in a state of inner frenzy. That way, you are easily manipulated.

Unfortunately, many people haven't learned how to decipher the messages and think everything they receive is for the highest good since it's from another dimension. Nothing could be further from the truth. Each dimension has Secret Flow and Bottom Sludge bandwidths of frequencies and unique receiving devices.

Remember all the ways we have received news and information over the past few years, phones, radios, TVs, videos, computers, cell phones, and microchips.

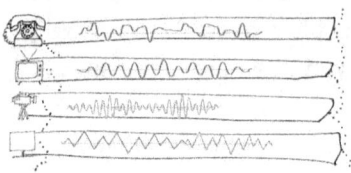

Each dimension has a different type of receiver/decoder. Pretend one dimension is like a TV connected to various money programs. One channel says you can get rich quickly by screwing others. Another program broadcasts your unworthiness, affirming that you will never be good enough. Another has a series devoted to following your feminine intuition and heart to build your joyous life. Or, you can turn the TV off, connect to your inner knowing, and have fun creating a new reality with your friends. You can tune in to the Bottom Sludge or the highest frequencies of each dimension.

Great discernment is needed. Guides appear to help you, but what is their message? Doom and gloom, warnings and fear, or practical advice? Your body knows the truth. Does your body relax, open, and feel joyful? Then, what you're receiving is your truth. Do you feel afraid, scrunched down, and tight, shallow breathing? Then it's not the correct information for you.

You are bombarded daily with waves of low frequencies. You can disconnect the low-frequency receivers and strengthen the reception of higher frequencies into your Soul Circuitry on every dimension. For example, Bottom Sludge receivers pick up fear, panic, doom, and gloom while siphoning off life force energy. Invite in Light Codes, Angels, and Secret Flow to assist in your disconnection process. Connect to your Soul Circuitry and invite frequencies that support your cells, nervous system, body, and spiritual awakening.

Imagine your body is held in a cocoon of safety, surrounded by a field of love and security so that your receivers only accept frequencies for your highest good on all dimensions, timelines, past, present, and future.

What level of information are you receiving? Do the full-body sway test described in Chapter 7. Your body knows the truth. Stay tuned to your body as you learn to decode the messages.

Top-Secret

For years I didn't know how to deal with the secrets of my family. I was afraid for anyone to see the depth of terror lurking inside, so I kept quiet and put up a false front. I was trained at an early age to hide what was going on. I started school when I was four, and my dad was off building the world's first hydrogen bomb, gone for over a year. I was told what to say, how to lie about my father.

My top-secret neural programming from my childhood helped me survive as an adult. After my spontaneous kundalini awakening when I was twenty-seven, I knew one thing for sure, to keep quiet. A few years later, I met a woman who had a similar spontaneous kundalini awakening, and she told her kids what was happening. They had her locked up in a mental institution; she was drugged, tortured with electroshock, put in a straight jacket, and locked up in a padded cell. She was a shell of a woman when I met her. When I heard her story, I was thankful I knew how to keep quiet. Luckily, today many people recognize the symptoms of a spiritual awakening, which was relatively unknown in the United States in 1973.

I never spoke up. I kept my thoughts, feelings, and ideas to myself. My friendships lacked depth because I was terrified to let people know me. Before I published my memoir, *Unseen Connections: A Memoir from Pain to Joy*,[1] my friends had no idea what I'd been through, how I thought or my inner knowledge. Writing my story made things concrete and tangible. It also brought the Nasties and bogeyman out of the closet into the light of day.

The cost of my family's secret prompting me to keep quiet kept me from speaking up about my work and gaining more clients and money —a favorable and unfavorable dichotomy. In the past, if I spoke about what I saw, I would be ridiculed, ostracized, and made wrong. But my silence also served me. In my years as a psychotherapist, my clients had an innate knowing the words they told me would never leave my lips.

Every family has its secrets, some more devastating than others. Victims of domestic abuse, incest, rape, and alcoholism are all humiliated into silence. Family secrets cloaked in shame and guilt permeate through the lineage. Family secrets have long-range costs, detriments, and consequences.

Years ago, I worked with a beautiful fifteen-year-old girl who had just been released from a drug and alcohol treatment center. She held family patterns of sexual abuse and believed her only alternative was to become a prostitute. During her sessions, she released her family abuse

The Inner (R)Evolution:

programming, uncovered her true nature, and her life changed dramatically for the better.

Seeing her profound transformation, one by one, over about three years, eleven of her family members came to see me. They each had been raped or incested and had never spoken about what had happened. No sharing of their experiences, helping each other through the trauma or devising ways to make the sexual abuse stop. Instead, riddled with guilt and shame, they kept silent. As a result, three generations of abuse, cloaked in secrecy, permeated the lineage. Generational patterns of trauma and abuse cleared.

Thirty years later, my original client found me on the Internet and thanked me for positively changing her life; she was thriving, happy, married, and a mother.

The survival patterns that assist in childhood also squish, contract, and deny who we are. Yet, tracking how our family patterns weave through our lives may reveal hidden gifts. Bringing the forbidden to the light, and seeing our family secrets' positive and negative aspects, opens the space for inner freedom and joy.

TIP:

Journal about secrets in your family system. What hidden trauma is ready to be reviewed and released? What are the negative and positive aspects of your family's secrets?

What if Your Fucked-up Parts are Your Hidden Gifts?

Planted and rooted in your inner mess are the seeds of your success and thriving. Those who have lived through traumatizing stuff are sitting on gold mines. Once the trauma is released and cleared, the deeper aspects of your brilliance are revealed.

What's happening in that jumble of junk creates your life. The pathway out of the neural debris is down and in. Spiral love and gratitude through all the horrors. Bring in your soul frequency to dissolve all your fears. Start clearing away the debris with love and gratitude.

The aspects you have judged are your gifts hiding under a stockpile of trash. Then, as you love all your messed-up parts, they transform. Your talents and aptitudes emerge. Like a sprout rising through thick cement, your brilliance awakes and blossoms.

Be gentle and loving with yourself. We tend to beat ourselves up in ways we never dream of hurting others. The key is to love yourself with more compassion and gentleness every day.

The amazing artist, Judy Chicago, states, "Truth is found in the ignored, the forgotten, and the left out." Have your inner mess be the compost that feeds and nurtures your dreams and desires. It takes great courage to look, but once you do, the rewards are profound.

The Inner (R)Evolution:

. . .

DEATH AND BIRTH

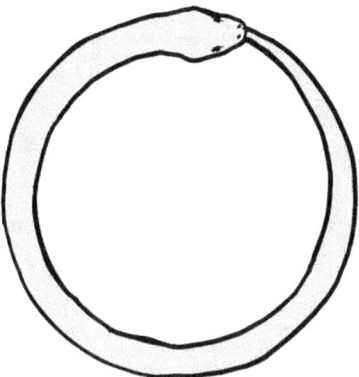

I've wanted to die for as long as I can remember. But it's forbidden.

The natural cycle of releasing the parts of me that I've outgrown is suppressed.

Fire surges up my spine; I invite in death. The flames dissolve the encrusted Fear Bot. Ancient trauma melts, flowing with ease and delight.

The taboo slides into pleasure. The pleasure of letting go of the old —the delight of no longer feeding and carrying the lies. The dying becomes more glorious. All the decaying aspects of the Fear Bot I held in my body are dying and leaving. Some of it is so old it's turned to dusty coal. It feels like layers of old clothes lifting from my body, old bodysuits of limitations, constriction, and who I'm supposed to be—delicious freedom, free of the shackles of the past, exploring the void of the deep feminine. I'm entering the mystery and the unknown.

My ecstatic soul essence fills all the spaces carved out by the dying structures. My body feels free, and new life flows. Joy bubbles from the deepest depths. Iridescent, luminous space for my multiple-dimensional selves continues to expand. Light Codes dance, angel wings flutter, gratitude vortexes swirl.

. . .

TIP:

Every new moon, and once a year during the Day of the Dead, clear out the painful crumbling of the Fear Bot. Give the old permission to dissolve and leave your body.

As a culture, Americans are afraid of death. We pretend it doesn't exist or believe it won't happen to us. Part of the natural cycle, death is contorted by fear.

Look at today's TV and movies filled with murder, torture, and crime. We are preoccupied with killing, violence, and pain. There is some part of us that is fascinated with death.

The old reality is dying, collapsing before our eyes. What's taking root are two radically different world views; a continuation of the old domination, power, and control or the birthing of the new reality of cooperation, generosity, and diversity.

What happens if we look from a different perspective? Instead of death lurking in the personal and collective unconscious, wreaking external havoc, what if we honor the natural cycle of death in our bodies?

The fear of death pervades, but who or what dies? The illusion dies, the thought forms perish, and the Nasties and implants expire. When the corrupt DNA codes dissolve, a massive inner death takes place. The lies discovered and new insights ignite unseen possibilities and glimpses of another reality. An organic process, death is a journey back into the void.

> Give your past lives freedom.
> Give your ancestors their liberation.
> Release all the deceased energies in your body.
> Explore your death and give it freedom.
> What wants to die and be reborn into something new?
> What are you willing to release into freedom?

Sovereignty

Your body, mind, and soul are yours; they don't belong to men, fathers, governments, or anyone. As you evolve, you claim sovereignty over your body, transforming fear and pain into innocent, joyous pleasure.

Sovereignty is having supreme power or authority, rightful status, independence, or prerogative. For this work, sovereignty is gaining control over your unconscious and hidden neural programs and the ability to clear up your corrupt DNA codes. The ultimate overseer, governance, the decision-making process to gain internal freedom from external control—the supreme power or authority over your own body to govern yourself.

We are taken over by foreign energies and the Fear Bot early on; we don't know what it's like to claim, love, and cherish our bodies. We've been duped for so long it feels forbidden to assert sovereignty over our bodies, minds, and souls.

Some neural programs and Nasties have been in your lineage forever, and they feel entitled to be in your body, feeding on your bones, blood, and life force.

Claim your life, not the projection of others—such a radical thought. We are on the cutting edge, creating a new humanity. The frequency of your body, aligned with your soul essence, creates a unified, coherent frequency that ripples through your life, the world, and the cosmos.

Incredible magic happens as you claim your body and take back your power. Your body and energy are yours; use them for your awakening into joy, play, and pleasure.

Power and Pleasure

It's easy to feel powerless with all that's happening in the world. We've seen how the current reality misuses power, so we become afraid. But fear keeps the old cycle going. Fun, enjoyment, and connecting to your mysterious gifts are prohibited. For many, pleasure is missing; like robots, we trudge through life, doing what we are supposed to do, powerless to change.

The distorted Fear Bot discounts and ridicules female power and pleasure. The pleasure pathway is usually cut off or blocked, the forbidden territory of the feminine, suppressed, tainted, and made wrong. We are commodities; the Fear Bot usurps our feminine energy in all dimensions.

You have been programmed to believe that you are powerless. The truth is that you hold a vast amount of power in your energy field. As you evolve, you learn how to use your energy. It's not about using your power willy-nilly. It's about upholding your deepest, soul-driven, heartfelt values. Not the dictates of society, religion, or politics, but use your authority to support your most profound truth.

So, where do you want to place your nourishing energy? Your

The Inner (R)Evolution:

energy has a tremendous impact on what flourishes and what dies from a lack of feminine power. Of course, we all have masculine and feminine energy. But only feminine energy brings life to babies, business, and everything that manifests on earth.

When you experience pleasure, fear and hopelessness evaporate, and your body feels safe, untapped brilliance and wisdom come to the surface. Safe to be you, safe to be seen. Full-body pleasure involves your brilliant mind, a generous, loving heart, and luscious, sensuous divine flow.

When your body is rooted in pleasure, you are present on earth, not in the clouds in your head. Pleasure is the grounding rod, the path to embodiment. The joy of being alive as you, soul essence flowing through you; this is the flowing power used to create a new reality.

Pleasure is feeling good in your skin, no matter what the current narrative would have you believe. Pleasure lubricates creativity, aliveness, and brilliant thinking. The most profound joy of feeling loved and safe in your skin—pleasure power, pregnant with possibility. Pleasure is the key to creating new realities. Fear, shame, and guilt are all designed to keep us cut off from pleasure, the divine feminine.

How can you incorporate more pleasure, joy, and satisfaction into your life? What wants your attention so it can manifest? What brings you the greatest joy? The pleasure of using your sacred life-giving erotic energy to create and birth all of your creations, when joined with your power, creates magical openings. Pleasure is the kiss of the beloved, your soul essence experienced in your cells and body.

PART IV
THE FINAL FRONTIER
UPSIDE DOWN

We are limited to the 3-D
and I refuse to believe that
bit by bit, awakening occurs
I realize this may be a shock, but
humanity's transformation is occurring
is a lie
people will blindly continue to follow the Fear Bot
don't tell me that

people can transform their DNA and neurology
because it looks like
humanity is doomed to extinction
I do not conclude that
we will joyfully thrive on multiple dimensions
In the future,
humanity will become robots, serving the Fear Bot
it no longer can be said that
our neurology creates our reality
it will be evident that
we can't change our reality
it is foolish to presume that
People will wake up and create a loving, inclusive reality for all.
And all of this will come true **unless we reverse it.**

— Dr. Cynthia Miller

And then, inside out, upside down, things are not as they seem. As your inner vision reveals your hidden wisdom, a surprising worldview emerges.

(the above poem read backward)

People will wake up and create a loving, inclusive reality for all.
it is foolish to presume that
we can't change our reality
it will be evident that
our neurology creates our reality
it no longer can be said that
humanity will become robots, serving the Fear Bot
In the future,
we will joyfully thrive on multiple dimensions
I do not conclude that
humanity is doomed to extinction

*because it looks like
people can transform their DNA and neurology
don't tell me that
people will blindly continue to follow the Fear Bot
is a lie
humanity's transformation is occurring
I realize this may be a shock, but
bit by bit, awakening occurs
and I refuse to believe that
We are limited to the 3-D.*

12. SPIRALING INTO FORM

The Movies

We live in a Fear Botland movie where we are the characters in a pre-programmed script. We are the genetically modified actors, unconsciously playing out a role in the matrix, imprinted with faulty neural programming and corrupt DNA coding. A multidimensional pixel light show that creates the 3-D you.

It's such a strange movie where the players live under a weird set of rules. We are replaceable cogs in a reality where our only purpose is to support a few people's wealth, power, and domination at the top of the pyramid. Fear and money rule.

It's a made-up movie we create every moment. We can keep playing the victim/perpetrator roles like the harried housewife, workaholic, flaky chick, macho dude, and woo-woo ding-bat. The list of pigeonholes goes on. Stuck in a box, reading your script, playing your part, hoping to escape. If you play your role well enough, you'll gain their freedom. That's not how it works.

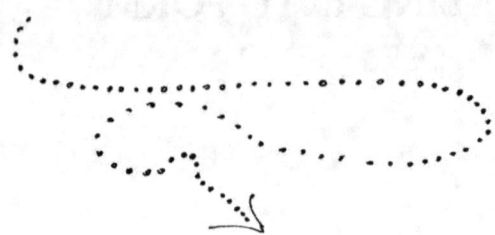

The Fear Botland loop keeps cycling through the dimensions, spiraling deeper creating a reality of loss of freedom and victimhood.

You can get out at any point in the cycle. Choose to create your path and play your heart-soul part as you go, bit-by-bit, day-by-day. Ask yourself, does this bring deep satisfaction, inner joy, and delight?

Pleasure is the path to escape Fear Botland. Fear keeps you stuck in your ancient reptilian brain. Pleasure opens all your senses, feelings, and intelligence. All of you as present to make the next exciting move along your path.

Welcome to the journey of your life. What is the game you choose to play? The choice is yours.

We each have our own game to play. How do you bring our joy, creativity, and brilliance to humanity to create a safe, sustainable, vibrant life for all?

See what your body has to tell you. My words are a trigger into the realms of cellular transformation. You have your own exciting, magnificent inner reality to explore.

You are here to create your own movie, where you are the star of your show. The part that only you can play, the meandering, unexpected, extraordinary path of your life. Experience the joy and the light of sharing your gifts with whomever you choose. Your gifts are the hidden mysteries, unknown and incomprehensible to the logical left brain.

The Inner (R)Evolution:

You are the movie producer and editor in charge of what scenes appear in your movie. Choosing your journey is the most remarkable thing you can do. So play around and see what feels lusciously delightful and follow that path. Throughout your day, keep following the direction of your inner knowing. You feel safe, held in the arms of love. You've created a home for all of your inner hurt little children. A place where all of you can play in the sun, splash in clean rivers, and love life. Change your world and life, filled with more joy, wild passion, and curiosity, flooding yourself with radiant drops of you.

Spiraling into Form

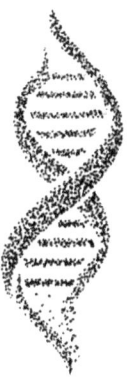

Space and time are alive. Our bodies and reality are spiraling into form. We are tapping into the past and future, dancing on a spiral, leaping timelines, gathering resources and wisdom, and bringing back information on creating a magical world for all based on love.

Things don't happen in the logical, linear order we are custom to in the 3-D reality of earth. Known as retrocausality in quantum theory, today's event could change the past just like the past influences the future.[1]

Timelines collapse, looking like an accordion closing. Sometimes it feels like you're riding a roller coaster and the images come fast while time collapses. Then, streaming threads of light release the Karmic Glue that kept us separated, divided, and opposed—magnetically repelling each other. Past, present, and future timelines collapse into one, here and now. Nothing is solid; we are vast space with a few molecules and atoms spinning around.

Light itself is consciousness. We are the universe, and the universe is us. The entire universe is intelligent, our every thought is connected with distant worlds.[2]

Your new DNA sequencing travels forward and backward through time and timelines. Your brilliance and consciousness traverse the cosmos. Your unique master DNA evolves and RNA carries out copies for the next thousands of years.

Your Multidimensional Business

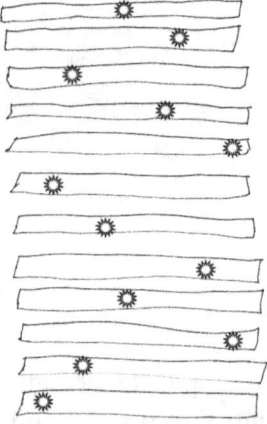

Creating a business is a remarkable way to fulfill your life's purpose, spread your vision, and be richly rewarded for sharing who you are. Your ideas, voice, and offers are needed.

How many health, social, financial, ecological, and political problems result from the Fear Bot's business model? A screwed-up system to enhance the wealth of a few while keeping the majority of the world in scarcity and poverty. The old way is to step on others to get to the top.

Divert your money from the old paradigm and the Fear Bot to the new reality. Build something radically different instead of patching up the leaky, corrupt system. The new business model is to share your light, like a searchlight beaming through the sky, calling people to follow your brilliant vision. Business is the way to make an impact.

Everyone's business is on a different dimension, depending on your soul's purpose, passion, and joy. Even though your business is located in one dimension, it incorporates all the other dimensions.

You may not have a clue about your business because it hasn't been invented yet. Like a tech start-up, your business is breaking ground, entering new territory that never existed before. Your business combines your multidimensional skills and talents, something only you can create.

For example, I'm the only one who could write this book; no one else has gone through the weird crap, magnificent, magical experiences, and life-threatening events I've experienced. Your life is just the same.

Weave together who you are on twelve dimensions to build a thriving, sustainable business. You are here to share the specialty that only you can make; it won't look like anyone else's.

Build a lifestyle that fits your Soul Circuitry. Not the lifestyle fed to us about who we should be, what to wear, and how to act. The artificial reality has nothing to do with who you are, what you love, and what makes you happy. A magical path where you decide what you want to change. What do you want more of, and what do you want to explore? Every facet of your business mirrors the Fear Bot in your body or the truth of who you are.

What do you see in the world that is not acceptable? What's your idea for changing it? How does the picture in your mind compare to the image you see in the world?

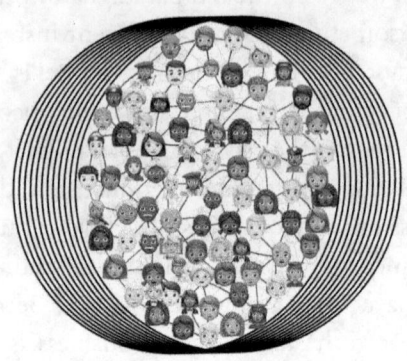

It's time to create the new; what's your vision? When a group of like-minded souls gathers, they create reality. We can stop feeding the chemical-based warmongering, hatred-producing Fear Bot. Instead, feed your joyful, expansive multidimensional self. The one that makes magic and experiences miracles. What reality does your radiant self choose?

We each have a piece to contribute to the new reality. But, like a jigsaw puzzle, the missing parts create a gaping hole of discontent, dissatisfaction, and inner angst.

As you rewire your cells, neural programs, and DNA, your life and business radically transform, opening more space for your Soul Self. Each breakthrough, insight, and moment of clarity opens an energetic space to hold more of your frequency.

The awakening happens in a community. We each spark ideas and inspiration to ignite hidden aspects of others and ourselves. The process of building your business is a reflection of your evolution, intertwining your vision and frequency.

It takes time to weave together twelve dimensions, a never-ending journey exploring the depths of who you are. Pieces emerge in order according to your essence. The next steps appear beyond logic or linear thinking, but according to unwinding the twelve dimensions of your joyful mastery. You've prepared for lifetimes for this moment. It's time to play big; the world needs your vision, clarity, expertise, and specific frequency.

. . .

The Inner (R)Evolution:

TIP:
You may want to re-read this book from the perspective of your business and take notes of the insights that arise.

ARE YOU READY TO BUILD YOUR BUSINESS, FOLLOW YOUR dreams, and face your fears? Release the Fear Bot's low-level consciousness business model and replace it with your soul's ecstatic, expansive all-inclusive frequency. The world needs your vision.

THE FINAL FRONTIER

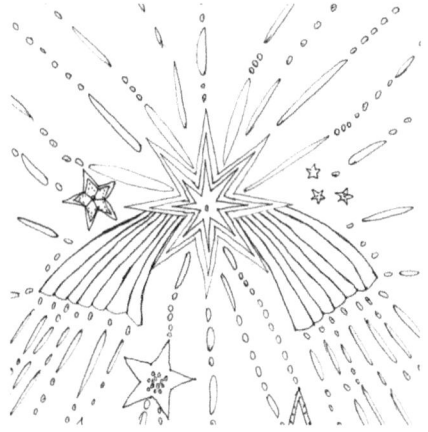

The collective unconscious manufactures a primordial soup filled with fear, anger, and hatred that runs our lives. Yet, few people are aware of the neurological process taking place. Currently, most people's internal programs support and feed the Fear Bot, the old paradigm, and patriarchy.

The old is surfacing, revealing who and what is pulling the strings. The lower vibrations elicit a world like a horror movie of the most wicked, treacherous, violent kind: sadistic delight, the power behind nuclear warfare, killing, and violence.

We've been programmed for eons to shut down our inner seeing, wisdom, and truth and only trust our logical left brain and outside authority. So unplug from your Childhood Circuitry and change your wiring from your seven-year-old. Your Soul Circuitry, a luscious, fractal, holographic structure, combines twelve or more dimensions and strands of DNA, reconfiguring the 3-D nervous system in your body.

Fear does not disappear; it takes on a new focus. Love meets fear, and the gremlins evolve, dissolve, or transform into allies. It's a magical process, not for the faint of heart but for people who want to experience life to the fullest.

We are each forging our way into unknown territory. The pandemic has shifted our world; now, we decide the outcome. We are in the dark. We see the next step; that's it, no long-range planning, no yearly spreadsheet with projects and potential earnings. In the trenches, one moment at a time. Moving in a spiraling, circular pattern, we pick up the necessary ingredients for the journey into the next step.

None of us can see the new yet; we've entered a time of possibility, a co-creation, not a world manipulated by a few, but something different that we have never known before.

Everything you've experienced in your life has prepared you for this glorious moment of freedom, inner joy, and luscious resolve.

When you realize you have the power, everything turns upside down. A delicious surrender leaves behind the Fear Bot and the limited 3-D and dissolves into a greater, more expansive you; this is the next step in human evolution, the exhilarating, joyful, scary journey into the unknown. Strip away the limitation and victim consciousness and claim your freedom through this joyous birthing process.

The mystical and practical unite in everyday life, not an out-of-body experience but a fully embodied reality. After a lifetime of wanting to escape the horror and terror of being human in your body, a depth of joy beyond the previous knowing radiates.

The Inner (R)Evolution:

People are waking up like little sprouts, and a grassroots revolution is occurring. Tiny seedlings worldwide manifest a vibrant, energetic ecosystem of a new humanity. A new world is opening; we create it with every breath. We sense it, feel it in our guts, know it in our deep wisdom, but the chaos and turmoil of the 3-D camouflage this new reality. When a critical mass of people wakes up, all of humanity rises to a higher, less dense frequency. Instead of a top-down existence with a few manipulating the outcome, the grassroots rebellion strengthens, demanding to be seen and heard.

Reread this book to grasp more depth into the big picture. Wake up to what's happening. Then, play with the Trailblazer Technologies and the Fear Bot. Discover what works for you. Become a trailblazer, forging your life's path and following your safe, loving soul rather than the tirades and manipulation of the Fear Bot. You can change your neural programs and DNA. You can do this.

Your unique DNA, dimensions, and frequencies contribute incredible and beautiful energies to this massive awakening. The Inner (R)Evolution is a journey to birth a new you and reality. Your genius becomes accessible here on earth, in your everyday life, moment by moment. Your Soul Self frequencies ripple out with each breath, inviting others to claim their hidden gifts.

Share your wisdom, passion, and love, anything else; you are ripping yourself off, selling yourself short, denying why you are here at this critical moment in the evolution of human consciousness.

The final frontier is to explore the depths of who you are, all dimensions and aspects of you—the surprising discovery of the freedom and joy of being you. It's time to play, shine your light, share your brilliance, and see what new reality you want to create. We each have our joyful luscious contribution to an amazing, safe, sustainable, healthy world for all filled with inner passion, pleasure, and fulfillment.

I offer this guidebook to you with my deepest love for your healing and evolution. Rewrite your story, and create your magical myth. Hiding under the Fear Bot and fog is the person you dream of becoming. And so, the adventure of self-empowerment continues.

Embark on this exciting, mysterious journey of profound awakening and evolution.

Claim who you are.
Create your new luscious reality!

ACKNOWLEDGMENTS

I am grateful to my parents for setting the stage for my incredible, miraculous life. The depth of my past ignited the spark to discover more profound truths.

Thank you, my writing cohorts Diane Osgood, Linda McLachlan, Kristin Dainis, Carolina Perez Sanz, and Kathy Karn, whose amazing support and encouragement were invaluable. I couldn't have done this book without you—so much gratitude to the Akimbo community and Kristin Hatcher, Seth Godin, and Writing in Community. Thank you for assisting me to claim my voice.

I sincerely thank Adam Gainsburg for his brilliant assistance.

Thanks to Christine Sheehy for her structural editing, helping me to get the book into a tangible form.

And thank you to my beta readers, Marilyn Driver and Ljuba Lemke, who so beautifully helped me with the book.

I give thanks to all my clients over the years. I'm so grateful to you for allowing me to assist in your awakening into a more joyous, fulfilling life. Thank you for trusting me with your deepest secrets to help your evolution. Thank you for supporting my journey of awakening and change. Your continued support has fueled this journey of discovery into freedom. I'm so grateful for each of you.

And finally, gratitude to you, dear reader, for reading and implementing the tools in the Inner (R)Evolution. Together, we can create a magical, amazing world for all.

With love,

Dr. Cynthia

GLOSSARY

Bottom Sludge: Bottom Sludge holds the Nasties: inner critic, self-sabotage, violence, hatred, and fear. Suckers and Takers, also found in the Bottom Sludge, are pathways or energetic patterns that consciously or unconsciously rob your energy.

Cell: One of the specialized units, consisting of the nucleus and protoplasm, composes the bodies of plants and animals. The primary activity of all cells is to transform energy.

Childhood Circuitry: Wired in your body by the time you are six, your Childhood Circuitry runs your life until you rewire your body to your Soul Circuitry. Your Childhood Circuitry is based on other people's ideas and beliefs about you and how you should live.

Corpus Callosum: The corpus callosum is the arched bridge of nervous tissue that connects the two cerebral hemispheres, allowing communication between the right and left sides of the brain.

Corrupt DNA Codes: Our corrupt DNA codes contain the despicable aspects of society, and create disease, while sexual abuse and violence patterns pass from generation to generation. In addition, the DNA code is prone to damage and mutations due to errors in DNA replication, free radicals, and radiation

Critical Mass: The minimum mass of fissionable material which can sustain a chain reaction.

Dream Builders: The second layer of the Soul Circuitry comprises 5th through 8th dimensions. Dream Builders birth the new reality through inner vision, love, and resources, including money.

Evolution: Changes in the genetic composition of a population during successive generations. The gradual development of more complex organisms from smaller, more simple ones.

Frequency: The number of completed cycles, waves, vibrations, etc., of a periodic phenomenon per second.

Grounding: Connecting with the earth to receive the earth's nurturing energy, release toxins, and connect who you are on multiple dimensions with the earth.

Healing Angels: The angels work on all aspects of the Fear Bot. They have your back and keep you safe and protected, a 9th dimension technology available to all. Anyone can call on the Healing Angels; you have direct access, and no intermediary is required.

Higher Self: Your Higher Self, associated with multiple belief systems, is an eternal, conscious, and intelligent aspect of you—the wise, unconditionally loving, creative, authentic inner you.

Implants and Brain Clamps: Another way the Fear Bot functions is through external apparatus wired in our bodies to keep us thinking and behaving in specific, prescribed routes.

Inner Freedom: The Soul Circuitry's third layer comprises 9th through 12th dimensions. This is where miracles, synchronicities, and connections to galactic families occur. Inner Freedom brings the cosmos' magic, wisdom, and mysteries into physical reality; they convey information to earth to help create a new reality and a new human.

Kali: The Divine Shakti represents the creative and destructive aspects of nature. Kali is the symbol of the dynamic power of eternal time, and in this aspect, she signifies destruction through which the seed of life emerges. She inspires terror in the parts of us that are not based in truth, and love in those parts of us that are...all at the same time.

Karma: The Hindu and Buddhist philosophy, according to which their behavior in this life determines the quality of people's current and future lives.

Kundalini: A powerful spiritual energy usually lying dormant in the physical body at the spine's base. Once carefully awakened, spiritual growth ensues.

Language of Your Cells: All processes in the body are based on conversations and group decision-making among cells.

Language of Your Soul: Your soul communicates with your body and cells in its unique language.

Light Codes: Magical packets of information, or quanta, light codes, eat the old toxic waste. They also bring in high-frequency information necessary for your evolution and transformation.

Limbic System: The Limbic System is in the middle part of the brain and involves human emotion regulation; it is concerned with emotions and instincts, feeding, and dogmatic and paranoid tendencies.

Matrix: The matrix, a part of the Fear Bot, is an energetic rigid structure of reality, broken down into tiny cubicles that create feeling alone, separate, unworthy, unloved, and not good enough.

Motherboard: The motherboard, the first layer of the Soul Circuitry, comprises the first four dimensions with stability, support, safety, and nourishment properties. Without this firm base and inner structure, the higher frequencies have nowhere to land.

Mudra: A mudra is a sacred finger movement; yogic control of specific organs helps concentration, which produces psychic responses.

Muscle Testing: A way of pinpointing any energy blockages in the body and communicating with the subconscious as clearly as possible.

Nasties: Nasties are despicable energies that sabotage, spread a lack of self-worth, and make us dislike ourselves.

Neural Programs: Our lives are influenced by how our neural programs operate. Triggering any part of the neural program creates a chain reaction throughout the body.

Neocortex: The newest part of the brain is concerned with speech, rational thought, and problem-solving. The neocortex affects creativity and the ability to learn.

Paradigm: A scientific model is a system to explain events in the field and is sufficiently open-ended to leave all sorts of problems resolved—a model or map of perceived reality.

Prana: A Hindu or yogic term used to describe the life force.

Quantum: Quanta, a discrete "packet" or unit of energy, angular momentum, or other physical quantities representing a minimum, indivisible quantity.

Glossary

<u>Reptilian Brain</u>: The reptilian brain acts on stimulus and response, is fear-driven, and is the oldest part of the brain.

<u>Samadhi</u>: The deep meditation, trance, superconscious state in which identification is realized: the final goal of yoga.

<u>Secret Flow</u>: The Secret Flow is the highest frequency of each dimension. The Secret Flow, a transmission beyond words, clears old trauma and debris, ignites creativity, and lusciously soothes the body. The Secret Flow, found within, is the path to inner freedom, joy, and peace.

<u>Shakti</u>: A Hindu term, Shakti is the Sanskrit term for the feminine energy of the divine. Shakti is the dynamic aspect of the Ultimate Principle, the power that permeates all creation, the foundational consciousness's energy.

<u>Shiva (Siva)</u>: Hindu god. In esoteric meaning, Siva is Pure Consciousness, the transcendent divine principle.

<u>Soul Circuitry</u>: The Soul Circuitry is the toroidal energy field framework for merging body and soul and remembering who you are. A multidimensional holographic living structure for the evolving human.

<u>Soul fragments</u>: The parts left behind when you incarnated in a body or the parts of you that left your body during a traumatic event.

<u>Soul Frequency</u>: The unique signature of who you are, the frequency or wavelength of your soul that emanates through your body.

<u>Soul Self</u>: Your body connected to your soul creates your Soul Self, similar to your Higher Self.

<u>Sovereignty</u>: Sovereignty is gaining control over your unconscious and hidden neural programs and the ability to clear up your corrupt DNA codes. The ultimate overseer, governance, the decision-making process to gain internal freedom from external control—the supreme power or authority over your own body to govern yourself.

<u>Spiraling Radical Gratitude and Love</u>: A process to shift lower energies by bringing in the high frequencies of gratitude and love.

<u>The Fear Bot:</u> The Fear Bot is the hidden inner mechanisms that feed the corruption, violence, and fear that runs rampant today. Some internal aspects included in the Fear Bot are corrupt DNA codes, sabotaging neural programs, and the matrix. The purpose of the Fear Bot is domination, manipulation, and control, and it is known as patriarchy and the old paradigm.

Trauma: Trauma is overwhelming situations, adverse events, or the shock of an accident. Trauma, a response to the past, is what happened to us; it's not who we are.

Veils of Illusion: The Veils of Illusion expose the current paradigm underbelly and reveal the forbidden, behind-the-scenes programming that makes up modern society.

Vibration: Vibrating motion or one unit of this, being a complete motion from a middle point out to one limit, then back through the central point to the other and back to the starting point again.

Wave: A time-varying quantity, which is also a function of position.

NOTES

2. Change Your Life and Reality

1. http://amazingastronomy.thespaceacademy.org/2022/09/the-real-matrix-physicist-says-our.html?fbclid=IwAR0Te5K90liFAzH99LI87yfj5SigzqLV8AB7VvZ0y_a56S4YKoq5Yc93M9o&utm_source=newsletter&utm_medium=email&utm_campaign=name_discovering_about_you&utm_term=2022-09-05
2. http://amazingastronomy.thespaceacademy.org/2022/09/the-real-matrix-physicist-says-our.html?fbclid=IwAR0Te5K90liFAzH99LI87yfj5SigzqLV8AB7VvZ0y_a56S4YKoq5Yc93M9o&utm_source=newsletter&utm_medium=email&utm_campaign=name_discovering_about_you&utm_term=2022-09-05

3. The Fear Bot

1. https://www.theclearingnw.com/blog/biology-of-belief-summary-dr-bruce-lipton-part-1
2. https://humansbefree.com/2017/12/proof-that-the-human-species-has-been-genetically-engineered-by-anunnaki-aliens.html
3. https://www.quantamagazine.org/the-complex-truth-about-junk-dna-20210901/
4. Miller, Cynthia, *The Art of Radical Gratitude,* https://www.drcynthiamiller.com/books
5. https://stanmed.stanford.edu/carla-shatz-vision-brain/#:~:text=Those%20results%20eventually%20led%20Shatz,up%2C%20while%20others%20are%20pruned
6. Norman Doidge, M.D., *The Brain That Changes Itself*, Penguin Books, 2007

4. Trailblazer Technologies and Soul Circuitry

1. Miller, Cynthia, *The Art of Radical Gratitude,* https://www.drcynthiamiller.com/books
2. Lieff, Jon, *The Secret Language of Cells,* Ben Bella Books, Dallas, TX, 2020.
3. Lieff, Jon, *The Secret Language of Cells,* Ben Bella Books, Dallas, TX, 2020.

5. The First Twelve Dimensions

1. https://nypost.com/2017/06/13/the-human-brain-sees-the-world-as-an-11-dimensional-multiverse/

Notes

6. The Motherboard

1. https://www.investopedia.com/ask/answers/030915/what-percentage-global-economy-comprised-oil-gas-drilling-sector.asp
2. https://www.investopedia.com/ask/answers/030915/what-percentage-global-economy-comprised-oil-gas-drilling-sector.asp
3. https://news.un.org/en/story/2022/06/1120662
4. https://www.cnbc.com/2022/02/16/big-oil-and-the-climate-crisis-the-fight-to-hold-pr-firms-accountable.html
5. https://www.investopedia.com/ask/answers/030915/what-percentage-global-economy-comprised-oil-gas-drilling-sector.asp
6. https://www.theguardian.com/business/2022/may/13/oil-gas-producers-first-quarter-2022-profits
7. https://www.pgpf.org/chart-archive/0053_defense-comparison
8. https://thehill.com/policy/defense/599997-biden-unveils-813-billion-request-for-fy-2023-defense-national-security-budget/
9. https://watson.brown.edu/costsofwar/papers/2021/ProfitsOfWar
10. https://watson.brown.edu/costsofwar/papers/2021/ProfitsOfWar
11. https://www.libraryofsocialscience.com/newsletter/posts/2015/2015-09-08-rak1.html
12. https://www.libraryofsocialscience.com/essays/koenigsberg-love-of-war/
13. https://www.libraryofsocialscience.com/newsletter/posts/2015/2015-03-06-hitler-lenin.html
14. https://knowledge4policy.ec.europa.eu/foresight/topic/changing-security-paradigm/world-military-expenditure_en
15. https://www.sipri.org/media/press-release/2022/world-military-expenditure-passes-2-trillion-first-time#:~:text=(Stockholm%2C%2025%20April%202022),2021%2C%20to%20reach%20%242113%20billion.
16. https://edition.cnn.com/2022/10/15/europe/russia-ukraine-rape-sexual-violence-military-intl-hnk/index.html
17. https://jill.substack.com/p/russians-are-using-rape-as-a-weapon
18. https://amp.theguardian.com/global-development/2022/dec/08/iranian-forces-shooting-at-faces-and-genitals-of-female-protesters-medics-say
19. https://amp.theguardian.com/global-development/2022/dec/08/iranian-forces-shooting-at-faces-and-genitals-of-female-protesters-medics-say
20. https://aeon.co/ideas/how-video-games-unwittingly-train-the-brain-to-justify-killing
21. https://aeon.co/ideas/how-video-games-unwittingly-train-the-brain-to-justify-killing
22. https://aeon.co/ideas/how-video-games-unwittingly-train-the-brain-to-justify-killing
23. https://www.coe.int/en/web/cyberviolence
24. https://explodingtopics.com/blog/number-of-gamers
25. https://www.bloomads.com/blog/is-mobile-game-advertising-right-for-you/
26. https://autonomousweapons.org/
27. https://autonomousweapons.org/
28. https://theconversation.com/un-fails-to-agree-on-killer-robot-ban-as-nations-pour-billions-into-autonomous-weapons-research-173616
29. https://blogs.scientificamerican.com/observations/rosalind-franklin-and-dna-how-wronged-was-she/
30. https://www.panna.org/key-issues/gmos-pesticides-profit

Notes

31. https://www.theguardian.com/environment/2018/jul/03/pesticides-are-good-for-profits-not-for-people
32. https://link.springer.com/article/10.1007/s10668-005-7314-2
33. https://foe.org/learn-truth-pesticide-companies/
34. https://www.newhallhospital.co.uk/news/is-sugar-more-addictive-than-cocaine
35. https://www.businesswire.com/news/home/20210730005355/en/Global-Weight-Loss-Products-and-Services-Market-Report-2021-A-377.3-Billion-Market-by-2026-with-8-CAGR-Forecast-During-2021-2026---ResearchAndMarkets.com
36. https://www.cdc.gov/nchs/products/databriefs/db313.htm
37. https://arstechnica.com/science/2019/01/healthcare-industry-spends-30b-on-marketing-most-of-it-goes-to-doctors/
38. https://arstechnica.com/science/2019/01/healthcare-industry-spends-30b-on-marketing-most-of-it-goes-to-doctors/
39. https://www.promarket.org/2022/06/29/healthcare-companies-spent-more-on-lobbying-than-any-other-industry-last-year/
40. https://www.statista.com/topics/1764/global-pharmaceutical-industry/
41. https://www.ncbi.nlm.nih.gov/pmc/articles/PMC3820993/
42. https://www.thereviewgeek.com/takeyourpills-xanax-moviereview/
43. https://www.forbes.com/sites/pamdanziger/2019/09/01/6-trends-shaping-the-future-of-the-532b-beauty-business/?sh=17fa294b588d
44. https://us.norton.com/blog/iot/how-facial-recognition-software-works
45. https://www.privacyworld.blog/2022/11/2022-q3-artificial-intelligence-biometric-privacy-report/
46. https://www.dailymail.co.uk/sciencetech/article-9271857/US-second-surveilled-country-China-one-camera-five-people-big-cities.html
47. https://www.gisreportsonline.com/r/war-on-cash/
48. https://pages.dataiku.com/ai-media-entertainment?utm_id=14310163377--128908357111--544388576101--ai%20in%20media&utm_source=nam-adwords&utm_medium=paid-search&utm_campaign=CONTENT%20AI%20in%20Media%20and%20Entertainment&gclid=Cj0KCQiAxbefBhDfARIsAL4XLRr9IeID8esO7Qwc6864u2-Y5knu-iDtT9BztyuFQeSeFK4udGk1G14aAk2PEALw_wcB
49. https://telecom.economictimes.indiatimes.com/news/global-artificial-intelligence-spending-to-reach-434-bn-in-2022/89701510
50. https://www.nytimes.com/2023/01/06/science/robots-artificial-intelligence-consciousness.html
51. https://futurism.com/the-byte/scientists-robots-move-mouse-muscles
52. https://www.yahoo.com/lifestyle/humanity-may-reach-singularity-within-110000706.html
53. https://www.freethink.com/robots-ai/voice-cloning-vall-e
54. https://www.theclearingnw.com/blog/biology-of-belief-summary-dr-bruce-lipton-part-1
55. https://www.theclearingnw.com/blog/biology-of-belief-summary-dr-bruce-lipton-part-1

7. Dream Builder

1. https://kathykarn.com/the-wisdom-of-elephants
2. https://www.outlookindia.com/international/the-long-shadow-of-british-colonialism-and-list-of-countries-once-part-of-british-empire-news-222475

Notes

3. https://www.natgeokids.com/nz/discover/history/general-history/british-empire-facts/
4. https://www.wearethemighty.com/articles/these-are-the-only-3-countries-america-hasnt-invaded/
5. https://www.wearethemighty.com/popular/countries-america-hasnt-invaded/
6. https://www.wearethemighty.com/popular/countries-america-hasnt-invaded/
7. https://www.washingtonpost.com/business/2022/03/12/lobbying-record-government-spending/
8. https://edition.cnn.com/2022/02/20/americas/canada-trucker-protest-covid-sunday/index.html
9. https://www.ohchr.org/en/women/sexual-and-reproductive-health-and-rights
10. https://www.nytimes.com/interactive/2022/us/abortion-laws-roe-v-wade.html
11. https://www.nytimes.com/interactive/2022/us/abortion-laws-roe-v-wade.html
12. https://www.kff.org/womens-health-policy/issue-brief/understanding-pregnancy-loss-in-the-context-of-abortion-restrictions-and-fetal-harm-laws/
13. https://www.nytimes.com/interactive/2022/us/abortion-laws-roe-v-wade.html
14. https://fee.org/articles/the-benefits-of-religion-are-more-than-spiritual/
15. https://www.theguardian.com/world/2016/sep/15/us-religion-worth-1-trillion-study-economy-apple-google
16. https://nubiapage.com/top-5-richest-churches-in-the-world-2022/
17. https://nubiapage.com/top-5-richest-churches-in-the-world-2022/
18. https://abuserefuge.org/is-sexual-abuse-declining-or-is-it-just-underreported/
19. https://www.business.com/articles/how-new-age-social-media-marketing-is-changing-and-what-you-need-to-know/
20. https://www.health.harvard.edu/medications/do-not-get-sold-on-drug-advertising
21. https://www.statista.com/statistics/953104/pharma-industry-tv-ad-spend-us/
22. https://www.statista.com/statistics/953104/pharma-industry-tv-ad-spend-us/
23. https://www.marketingmind.in/worlds-largest-advertisers-in-2021/
24. https://futurism.com/the-byte/amazon-pays-spy-phone-traffic
25. https://futurism.com/scientists-marketers-ads-dreams
26. https://futurism.com/scientists-marketers-ads-dreams
27. https://aeon.co/essays/dreams-are-a-precious-resource-dont-let-advertisers-hack-them
28. https://blog.hootsuite.com/social-media-advertising-stats/
29. https://www.digitalmediastream.co.uk/blog/the-2022-social-media-stats-report
30. https://www.ncbi.nlm.nih.gov/pmc/articles/PMC7215249/
31. Miller, Cynthia, *The Art of Radical Gratitude*, 2007, https://www.drcynthiamiller.com/books.
32. https://www.cnbc.com/2018/04/10/today-isnt-equal-pay-day-for-black-latina-or-native-american-women.html
33. https://www.cnbc.com/2018/04/10/today-isnt-equal-pay-day-for-black-latina-or-native-american-women.html
34. https://www.cnbc.com/2018/04/10/today-isnt-equal-pay-day-for-black-latina-or-native-american-women.html
35. https://www.youtube.com/watch?v=vk7_2zpaygE
36. https://www.jpmorganchase.com/news-stories/cbriggs-closing-the-womens-wealth-gap
37. https://www.jpmorganchase.com/news-stories/cbriggs-closing-the-womens-wealth-gap
38. https://www.theceomagazine.com/business/finance/richest-family-walton-walmart/
39. https://www.theceomagazine.com/business/finance/richest-family-walton-walmart/

40. https://www.cnbc.com/select/us-credit-card-debt-hits-all-time-high/
41. https://www.insidermonkey.com/blog/5-biggest-industries-in-the-world-in-2021-925230/5/
42. https://www.visualcapitalist.com/where-worlds-banks-make-money/
43. https://robertreich.substack.com/p/the-three-myths-used-by-the-ultra?r=df4tg&utm_campaign=post&utm_medium=email&fbclid=IwAR2Sc_D1c1dItLIEfornuHz0sa5zwBinY7pnxXCF55bDBKRUHCxwZ4iwaE#details
44. https://robertreich.substack.com/p/the-three-myths-used-by-the-ultra?r=df4tg&utm_campaign=post&utm_medium=email&fbclid=IwAR2Sc_D1c1dItLIEfornuHz0sa5zwBinY7pnxXCF55bDBKRUHCxwZ4iwaE#details
45. https://www.nytimes.com/2018/12/03/us/politics/fact-check-pentagon-medicare-alexandria-ocasio-cortez.html
46. https://www.nytimes.com/2018/12/03/us/politics/fact-check-pentagon-medicare-alexandria-ocasio-cortez.html
47. https://www.nytimes.com/2018/12/03/us/politics/fact-check-pentagon-medicare-alexandria-ocasio-cortez.html
48. https://www.cnbc.com/2017/01/16/the-worlds-eight-richest-people-have-same-amount-of-money-as-half-the-world-oxfam.html
49. https://www.un.org/en/un75/inequality-bridging-divide#:~:text=In%202018%2C%20the%2026%20richest,exacerbating%20within%20-country%20income%20inequality.
50. Diane Osgood, Ph.D., *Your Shopping Superpower*, https://dianeosgood.com/shopping-superpower/
51. https://www.drcynthiamiller.com/books

8. Inner Freedom

1. https://www.npr.org/sections/thetwo-way/2018/02/21/587671849/a-new-survey-finds-eighty-percent-of-women-have-experienced-sexual-harassment
2. https://www.ucanews.com/news/covid-19-pandemic-fuels-rise-in-sexual-abuse/95790
3. https://www.rainn.org/statistics
4. https://www.rainn.org/statistics
5. https://www.drcynthiamiller.com/books
6. https://www.rainn.org/statistics/victims-sexual-violence
7. https://www.un.org/en/un75/inequality-bridging-divide#:~:text=In%202018%2C%20the%2026%20richest,exacerbating%20within%20-country%20income%20inequality.

11. Exploring Deeper

1. https://www.drcynthiamiller.com/books

12. Spiraling into Form

1. https://www.academia.edu/40879212/Backward_Causation_Epistemological_Issues_and_Metaphysical_Implications_Tesi_Magistrale_Bologna_

Notes

2. https://www.reddit.com/r/whatistrue/comments/ye33z4/the_entire_universe_is_intelligent_our_every/

ABOUT THE AUTHOR

Dr. Cynthia Miller is a visionary, alchemist, and evolutionary change agent. In 1973, after a near-death experience, a jolt of energy shot from her lower back into her head. From one breath to the next, her life radically changed. She experienced weird seeing, strange happenings, and saw energy, inside bodies, and cells. Confused and disoriented, she became aware of other realms and inner knowing. Four years later, she learned that she had experienced a spontaneous kundalini awakening.

To discover what she was perceiving and living, she received a Ph.D. in Cellular Transformation and the Psychology of Change in 1985. The magical, mystical, and scientific merged with everyday life. Since then, Dr. Cynthia has worked with thousands of clients to bring more happiness, self-worth, and fulfillment into their lives.

Dr. Cynthia's passion is to guide others through the vast unknown to connect with their wisdom, explore who they are, and embody their unique contribution to the world. This self-empowerment adventure leads to feeling worthy, inner freedom, love, and joy.

A mystic storyteller, her books include *Unseen Connections: A Memoir from Pain to Joy*, *The Art of Radical Gratitude*, and *I Am Worthy: Ignite Your Feminine Power - Self-Help Adult Coloring Book*.

DrCynthiaMiller.com

facebook.com/cynthia.miller.16940

instagram.com/dr_cynthia

youtube.com/DrCynthiaMiller

www.ingramcontent.com/pod-product-compliance
Lightning Source LLC
Chambersburg PA
CBHW071900290426
44110CB00013B/1227